Published in association with
Centre for Information on Langua

Using technology in language learning

Edited by Stephen Hagen

Number 7 in a series of CTC Trust publications
General Editor Dr Helen Sharp

Previous titles in this series, available from the CTC Trust:

1. *Curriculum and resources: computer provision in a CTC* by Lawrence Denholm,
   ISBN 1 873882 00 9;
2. *Keyboard proficiency: an essential skill in a technological age* by Eve Gillmon,
   ISBN 1 873882 01 7;
3. *The foreign language needs of British business* by Stephen Hagen,
   ISBN 1 873882 06 8;
4. *Business education in the secondary school: a CTC response* by Eve Gillmon,
   ISBN 1 873882 08 4;
5. *The longer school day and five term year in CTCs: some initial observations*
   by Julia Hagedorn, ISBN 1 873882 09 2;
6. *Post-16 provision in CTCs: bridging the divide*
   by Ruth Jones, ISBN 1 873882 07 6.

This series of publications is intended to disseminate within the educational arena in this country and abroad, the information, expertise and experience emerging from CTCs. CTCs are independent colleges; within national guidelines each is free to develop the CTC initiative in its own way. The CTC Trust respects this independence and wishes to state that its publications do not necessarily reflect the policy or practice of the movement as a whole.

Published in Great Britain by City Technology Colleges Trust Limited in association with Centre for Information on Language Teaching and Research.

First edition April 1993.

Printed by Rustin Clark, Waterloo Road, Cricklewood, London NW2 7TX.

Cover photograph supplied by Acorn Computers Ltd, Cambridge.

ISBN 1 874016 08 9

City Technology Colleges Trust Limited,
15 Young Street,
London W8 5EH.

Charity No. 296729

Centre for Information on Language
Teaching and Research,
20 Bedfordbury,
London WC2N 4LB.

Further copies of this publication may be obtained from CILT Mail Order, P.O. Box 8, Llandysul, Dyfed SA44 4ZB.

Preface

At the National Council for Educational Technology, we are well aware of the potential value of using technology in learning generally, and in particular, in language learning. We have undertaken considerable work in this area in partnership with others such as the National Curriculum Council and welcome this book as yet more evidence of what can work, and how.

Even when learning through technology is well proven and the results published, it may still not be implemented. There are many reasons for this, but one of them is that the technology must be presented to teachers in schools as a solution to problems rather than yet another problem. The increased emphasis on language learning in schools is undoubtedly creating problems on which technology can be targeted. We would not suggest that technology can replace all other types of language learning, but when fully integrated it can provide a powerful tool to enhance learning. In order to be a solution, the technology must be targeted on the curriculum and be easily integrated into planned programmes of work, it must be easy to use, readily available, and complement the role of the teacher.

The continuing advance of technology is particularly important as applied to language learning. Although very exciting and valuable work can be achieved with existing technology, there is no doubt that the integration of sound and moving pictures into computers will open up new opportunities and possibilities for children learning languages. The video clips which will be possible will allow learners to interact with language taking place in a variety of contexts in different locations. This brings a dimension into the curriculum that is very difficult to replicate without the technology. It is extremely important that as these powerful technologies emerge, they should be designed in such a way that far from being more complex to use they are easier to use. The technology must fade into the background allowing the learner to concentrate on the learning.

Technology also opens up possibilities for flexible, autonomous learning. In this way, the learners begin to develop their own successful learning strategies; hence in addition to increasing their skills in language, they will also be increasing their ability to learn.

We welcome the work of the CTC Trust and look forward to working with them in promoting the appropriate use of technology in learning languages.

Margaret Bell,
Chief Executive, National Council for Educational Technology

Table of contents

Glossary

The following abbreviations are used in this document:

AAC   Audio-active-comparative;
AoE   Area of Experience (National Curriculum);
BLC   Brealey Languages Centre;
BTEC   Business and Technology Education Council;
CALL   Computer-assisted language learning;
CBT   Computer-based training;
CD   Compact disk;
CD-i   Compact disk interactive;
CD-ROM   Compact disk read only memory;
DES   Department of Education and Science (renamed DfE July 1992);
DfE   Department for Education;
DTP   Desk Top Publishing;
DVI   Digital Video Interactive;
EC   European Community;
FLAW   Foreign languages at work;
FLIP   Flexible Language Instruction Program;
GNVQ   General National Vocational Qualification;
GOML   Graded Objectives for Modern Languages;
INSET   Inservice Training;
IT   Information Technology;
IV   Interactive video;
KS3   Key Stage 3 (National Curriculum);
KS4   Key Stage 4 (National Curriculum);
LCCI   London Chamber of Commerce and Industry;
MFL   Modern foreign languages;
NALA   National Association of Language Advisors;
NCC   National Curriculum Council;
NVQ   National Vocational Qualification;
SOBA   Schools Olympus Broadcasting Association;
TSI   Technology in Schools Initiative;
TVEI   Technical and Vocational Education Initiative;
UBI   Understanding British Industry;
VCR   Video Cassette Recorder.

Introduction

Stephen Hagen, CTC Trust

The advent of multimedia and, in particular, the affordable addition of sound and moving video to the desk-top computer, looks set to revolutionize language learning technologies before the end of the century. Despite the technological uncertainties, many schools and colleges in England and Wales are currently having to upgrade their hardware and software provision in line with the requirements of the National Curriculum and the GNVQ framework. Given timetable restrictions, plus insufficient numbers of languages staff to meet demand, there is also a widespread expectation that technology can fill the gap. Indeed, there is little doubt in most language teachers' minds that the use of technology – from cassettes to satellites – can enhance language learning and contribute to better performance. It has already been used successfully in support of the curriculum, as well as in independent learning at many levels of education.

Technology is not, however, a universal panacea, or complete substitute for a teacher. Fewer than 20% of adults, for example, ever get very far in autonomous technology-based learning without any tutorial support. There are also pitfalls in choosing the right technology and integrating it into the curriculum and into a new physical environment. This book addresses many of these issues from a practical viewpoint and, hopefully, answers the questions uppermost in most practitioners' minds: what works, how much does it cost and where do you put it?

This book is basically intended for decision-makers in schools and colleges, individual teachers and language consultants who wish to introduce new technology into the Modern Languages curriculum. It comprises a set of practical models of how technology has been successfully integrated into the curriculum and married to students' learning needs. The chapters have been written by the practitioners themselves who oversaw the development of the language-learning technology in a learning environment. They are themselves teachers of languages and able to speak in practical down-to-earth terms, based on experience, rather than just from a theoretical standpoint.

At the strategic level, the key issue for many schools is how to deliver the National Curriculum in Modern Languages to a broader constituency of students and introduce entitlement and Modern Language GNVQ modules into the post-16 phase. Within this context, the questions are: At what level, and to what extent, can technology be introduced in support of these aims?

What is an appropriate methodology? What are the costs? How quickly will today's technology become obsolescent in view of accelerating technological change? Above all, how effective is a technology-based approach to language learning?

The book details the models, specifications and broad costs of systems operating in a range of different institutions with varying levels of finance. It is full of ideas, including solutions to problems, as well as the rationale for selecting certain systems over others. In the appendices there is additional practical information on costings, lists of equipment and various plans of language centres, including furnishing, and further examples from other institutions of using satellite and a voicecard language laboratory.

The contributors and their contributions

The schools featured in the main body of the book are all secondary, taken from different areas with different histories and various levels of funding. They are:

1. George Stephenson Community High School – an LEA-controlled high school in Tyne and Wear;

2. St George's School, Sleaford – a grant-maintained, Technology School in Lincolnshire, affiliated to the CTC Trust;

3. Djanogly CTC – Nottingham's CTC, opened in 1989;

4. Thomas Telford School, Telford – a CTC, opened in September 1992.

Each uses a variety of hardware and courseware resources and has developed different approaches to learning languages through technology.

Each case study follows a particular theme:

Chapter I: Flexible learning using a range of technologies (George Stephenson High School);

Chapter II: Upgrading an existing centre with PC 386s (St. George's School);

Chapter III: Integrating multimedia technologies within a Tandberg IS10 suite (Djanogly CTC);

Chapter IV: Researching and Developing the Digital Language Laboratory (Thomas Telford School).

The rationale for selecting schools has been to identify schools at different stages of development in the use of technology. George Stephenson Community High, for example, has been at the fore of Flexible Learning in Modern Languages for several years and was involved in the National TVEI Flexible Learning project; the Brealey Languages Centre at St. George's has just completed a programme of refurbishment and re-equiping; the Communications Centre at Djanogly is purpose-built and one of the best equipped and longest established of CTC language centres, having pioneered multimedia language applications at secondary level; and Thomas Telford School is the UK site for the development of the EC LINGUA-supported ELOQUENT project which will develop a networked digital language laboratory and pilot interactive courseware for post-16 modern language students.

Each of the contributors has not only been directly involved in planning and implementing the languages curriculum, but also in making purchasing decisions. Each has been the architect of the approach set out in the chapters of the book. The contributors' main objective is to describe, rather than prescribe, models to others. In so doing, they nonetheless highlight many of the practical issues facing language departments today.

Apart from Chapter IV, which is concerned with ELOQUENT, a multimedia research and development project, each of the contributors follows a similar pattern. They describe the origins of, and rationale for their language centres, or facilities; the role of technology in the curriculum; how they have designed their language centre, or suite, (its layout, specification and support infrastructure), the hardware and software they bought (i.e. suitable CALL software programs, including authorware) and, where applicable, how they have integrated the 'newer' technologies, such as electronic mail, video distribution, or satellite, with the 'older' audio-active-comparative (AAC) functions. The chapters also raise practical issues that every school or college faces in seeking to select the best, i.e. most effective and up-to-date, language learning facilities from the many available options.

The appendices contain a wealth of material from a range of sources: a short bibliography of multimedia materials, technical specifications, costings, guidance notes from the National Curriculum Council, a section on using satellites from Brooke College, Corby, example room layouts for language centres and suites from NALA and Dereham Neatherd High School, Norfolk, and descriptions of the latest audio-active-comparative lab and an experimental voicecard language laboratory set up in Wales. The final appendix contains a review of current multimedia platforms.

Rationale for using technology in language learning

The requirements of the National Curriculum

Much of the rationale for introducing technology into the languages curriculum comes from the demands of the National Curriculum. The general requirements for the MFL Programmes of Study state that 'All pupils should have opportunities in both Key Stages 3 and 4 to develop information technology capability' (DES/WO/HMSO, 1990a). Although IT is only one aspect of technology, the particular emphasis given to IT ensures that any new hardware resourcing of the MFL curriculum will have to include computers.

The *Modern Foreign Languages Non-Statutory Guidance* (NCC, 1992, F1) recognizes the contribution that IT can make to language learning by:

- giving ownership to pupils by enabling them to create, store and retrieve their own information in the target language in a way which they perceive as interesting and of value;

- extending the range of reading and writing activities;

- encouraging active use of the target language;

- providing opportunities to build up fluency;

- encouraging creativity because of the ease with which changes can be made to written documents and the professional way in which they can be presented;

- promoting a sense of accuracy;

- offering opportunities to explore structure and grammar in ways appropriate to a wide range of language learners.

Table 17 of the Guidance (see Appendix D) identifies key statements within the Programmes of Study for Technology (AT5, DES/WO/HMSO, March 1990b) which have links with the MFL programmes of study. Clearly, it is possible for schools to interpret the National Curriculum for Modern Languages with a strong technological focus, which has been the tendency of the schools in this book. Two specific uses are highlighted in the non-statutory guidance:

- access a database of press articles or commercial information, e.g. using CD-ROM or online database;

- use text manipulation software to practise structures and develop a range of vocabulary. (NCC, 1992, F3).

In the section *Working with IT* (NCC, 1992, F4), the Guidance continues,

Departments will need access to the following types of hard or software if they are to provide a variety of opportunities for pupils, both in terms of IT and MFL experience: Word-processing... Desktop publishing... Database...Communications Software...Text manipulation software... Concept keyboard.

Can language learning be enhanced by computer-based technology?

The primary pitfall facing teachers and educational planners is the temptation to place the technology before the student and so make inaccurate assumptions about the links between the learning process and the use of the technology underpinning it. In modern languages there is a real danger here, for the benefits that the new technologies can bring to language teaching are, in theory, abundantly evident, enabling the learner to access a wealth of live foreign language material and cultural information from abroad through a variety of systems ranging from electronic mail and satellite to computer-assisted language learning (CALL). The speed of their arrival on the scene, however, has left many language teachers breathless at the number of possibilities opening up before them (provided they have the resources!), yet still unsure of how effective the new technology can really be in enhancing learning and how, and in what measure, technology can replace direct face-to-face language teaching in the classroom.

There is, unfortunately, a dearth of sound empirical research into the relationship between second language acquisition and the use of technology on which to base decisions. The application of new technologies to language learning is happening with such an urgency and rapidity that few can predict its impact on the established teaching methods of the seventies, such as the communicative approach, and even fewer have had time to evaluate the effectiveness of technology-based methods on rates of language learning.

Where research exists (which is largely in Higher Education), it has tended to concentrate either on the materials supply side (specification and design issues, or state-of-the-art surveys), or on developing methodological models. In particular, there is little empirically-based observation of how students learn a second language with a computer, i.e. which learning strategies they employ at different ages and stages of learning. The open learning technology that suits a business person in a company is rarely appropriate to young people in schools and colleges.

Two recent initiatives from the National Council for Educational Technology to evaluate general CD-ROM applications in schools and, more specifically, pilot the *Vektor Connections* series of interactive language learning laserdisks should, however, shed light on whether or not the impact of technology on learning can be measured in any meaningful way. But for the time being, teachers have only the experience and recommendations of others to draw on and, in this respect, the case study material in the book, written by experienced practitioners in language teaching, should provide a helpful source of practical information and ideas.

What is the state of multimedia language learning technology?

Language learners did not start to benefit from the revolution in new technology until recently when sound, text and pictures could be combined in a single multimedia program on laserdisk, or on CD-ROM, or generated from inside a single box by software, such as in the case of the 'multimedia computer'. There are now systems on the market which can genuinely be called 'multimedia computers', such as the Acorn Archimedes (A5000 and A540 series) with RISCOS 3 (ARM3 chip) and *Replay*, running *GENESIS II*, or *Avanti*, and the Apple Macintosh LC with 4 mb of RAM (a minimum 68020 processor, preferably with a Video RAM [VRAM] upgrade) with *QuickTime*.

More recently, the 'multimedia PC' has appeared on the market for around £2000 (+ VAT) with the following minimum specifications: 386sx 25 Mhz (2 mb RAM, SVGA graphics), 40 mb HD, CD-ROM drive, 3.5" 1.4 mb floppy drive, Soundblaster Pro DA/MIDI, serial and parallel port, *MS-Windows 3.1*, mouse, headphones, 14" SVGA monitor and keyboard. With the emergence of low-cost digital systems, it is unlikely that current analogue systems, i.e. interactive video (IV) courseware running on a laserdisk player attached to a computer, will survive on the open market for much longer than two more years. Currently, the standard analogue-based interactive video workstation costs around £4000 and comprises, for example, an IBM PS/1 PRO 386 computer (20 Mhz, 80 mb Hard drive), laserdisk player 3300, voice record kit with Soundblaster card and a DVA 4000 overlay card with VGA card. The add-on hardware, e.g. laserdisk player, required for analogue systems adds not only to the expense, but makes the system cumbersome and inconvenient to handle.

It does, however, have the major advantage of high quality video pictures, but it is only a matter of time before the cost of digitizing moving video falls and the quality increases.

Multimedia language learning courseware is still in its infancy, however (see Chapter IV), and few programs of a pedagogic quality that would please a language teacher in a formal educational environment are currently on the market. Several do, however, provide potentially interesting interactive language learning models where the approach and materials design features could be adapted for group teaching on a computer network. Worth noting, in this respect, are

1. The *Vektor Connections* series for adults learning business languages (French, English, German, Italian, Spanish and Japanese), which run on a stand-alone system using the analogue video workstation technology with moving video described above.

2. MLS/Hodder and Stoughton's *Hotel Europa* multimedia CD-ROM for French, German and Spanish, costing £80 per CD-ROM. Only stills and graphics are used and a 386 IBM-compatible computer is needed with VGA display, 640k of RAM, 5 mb free on a local hard disk and a CD-ROM drive with audio output facility.

The potential of compact disk technology

Although in its infancy, CD-ROM technology appears to offer great potential to language learners. The major obstacles are the costs of using it with classes of learners studying simultaneously in a group situation (each would need a CD-ROM drive) and the level of interactivity achieved in a system which is 'read only', i.e. students cannot write (save) information to it. Recording the student's voice would therefore have to be done separately, using a cassette recorder, or voice card and local hard disk. Nonetheless, there are increasing numbers of CD-ROMs containing language material and courses. The advantages are cheapness and mass storage capacity.

Each disk stores the equivalent of 1500 5.25" floppies, i.e. it can hold 72 minutes of stereo sound, 16 hours of speech quality mono sound and 250,000 pages of A4 text (equivalent to the UK's 90 telephone directories on one disk). But only one minute of full-motion video material (9000 stills) can be stored on all this capacity and this would take about two hours to process and display without compression and decompression routines. The question then arises: how important is it to have moving pictures and the opportunity to record, or save, a student's own input?

There is, moreover, a burgeoning sector of new disk-based consumer-oriented digital technologies (CD-i, CDTV) which are designed for self-managed learning at home on a single-system basis. Both of these systems, which are being heavily marketed on the High Street, can be used for language learning, though they are currently accessed through the domestic television set and controlled by a joystick. Student input is not intended, though it could be built in separately with the addition of a user-controlled cassette recorder. The prospect of a new mass consumer market for CD-i materials may well lead to an upsurge in new 'interactive' language courses designed to run on the television at home.

The technology is impressive, but can it be used in schools in such a way that it adds value to the sum of the existing language learning technologies? Clearly, until models have been developed for integrating these systems and their courseware into the curriculum, a flexible learning approach mixing and matching technologies to achieve the best results would be the only way forward. Students would access each of these technologies as part of a learning plan devised by the teacher. Currently, they would have to work in small groups and additional 'low-tech' material would have to be developed to enable the teacher to make an assessment.

Designing technology-based courseware

It would be unwise to assume that the courseware for these systems is appropriate to the needs of groups of different learners at various ages in the classroom or that more could be learned in the time available than would be achieved from using lower-cost well-established systems, such as video or audio tape, with back-up exercises. There is a dilemma here. Most busy teachers would prefer off-the-shelf packages which meet the class's learning objectives without too much preparation of additional materials. However, few packages exist which satisfy specific class demands. Programs designed for the adult business market would generally be adaptable to post-16 schemes, studying courses such as those of FLAW, BTEC or LCCI, but are of less value lower down the school with larger and sometimes less mature classes. It will be some time before a full range of high quality truly interactive materials exists for use in schools.

Nonetheless, the advantage of the multimedia computer-based approach is that students and teachers themselves can develop their own multimedia materials on a content-free authoring package like *GENESIS II* (for Archimedes), *ToolBook, Authorware Professional, GENESIS III for Windows,* or *Linkway* (for IBM-compatibles) and *HyperCard* and *SuperCard* (for Apple Mac). Indeed, language teachers in Thomas Telford School, Djanogly CTC and St. George's School are already compiling their own multimedia materials, as, in fact, are many other teachers around the country.

Is the language laboratory effectively dead?

Computer networks are already gradually replacing the old-style cassette-based AAC language laboratories. Although the technology already exists for a multimedia language laboratory, the costs are still too high and the quality, i.e. the resolution, of low-cost digitized moving video is still too unimpressive. Even if it improves in the short term, for the vast body of schools, there will be a strong argument for sticking with the older, and often cheaper, more established cassette-based technologies for a while longer, and seeking to experiment with multimedia on a small scale within the computer centre. In the medium term, CD-ROM players look to be a good investment, too, and the number of language learning programs available for them will grow.

In the medium to long term, language centres will be digital, rather than analogue. Tape and laserdisk-based language materials will ultimately be replaced by floppies, probably magneto-optical disks, CD-ROMs and CD-i programs with moving colour video, sound and text and the console will house a file-server. In some cases, students will often not be aware of the source of the program, but simply load it directly from the hard disk. Digital laboratories are a reality today, as in the case of Thomas Telford School, and in Appendix J.

The ELOQUENT project described in Chapter IV provides a useful example of what is currently possible. It has developed a discrete Archimedes-based multimedia network, run off the main PC network, capable of downloading language learning programs with high quality sound, quarter-screen VGA-quality digitized moving colour pictures. *GENESIS II* pilot applications are being developed by teachers and it is hoped that students will soon be able to author their own interactive applications for others to use.

Resourcing the language centre

The size of capital budget for equipment purchases can vary substantially from one school to another. Moreover, the popular assumption that the rate of language learning in a class is directly proportional to the level of capital spending on a language centre is, I believe, unsubstantiated, since the contributors make it clear that there are too many other critical factors in successful language learning for this hypothesis to hold true in every case. In particular, staff and student motivation, the quality of teaching and the level of openness by both staff and students to using technology are significant variables.

The cost of setting up modern computer-based language learning facilities from scratch today is very high (see Appendix C) and may seem out of reach. However, the facilities described in this collection have, for the most part been built up over several years, and the price of computer hardware is dropping continually. To put things into perspective, the price of buying and installing a 12-workstation network of multimedia computers, able to handle sound and video, is now little more than a sophisticated AAC language laboratory of the same size. Moreover, a computer network can be more versatile: two or more can engage in pair work at a computer workstation more easily than in the standard language laboratory and the network can also be used for subjects other than languages.

None of the schools featured here could have achieved the success it has, were it not for actively, and persistently, seeking external sponsorship specifically for developing modern languages facilities. Indeed, the schools in the book have developed their exceptional facilities without imposing an undue burden on school finances.

George Stephenson School received sponsorship from British Telecom, TVEI, several European programmes (especially LINGUA) and has acquired ICL sponsorship which started in January 1993. The Brealey Languages Centre at St George's School was endowed by Reg Brealey, a local businessman and Chairman of the Governors, in 1985. A local Nottingham businessman, who is the main sponsor of Djanogly CTC, Sir Harry Djanogly, has given particular support to the Communications Centre, which has also received help from Tandberg. The ELOQUENT project at Thomas Telford School is supported by a combination of EC funding from the LINGUA programme, including a proportion of funding from Acorn Computers Ltd., and support and sponsorship from the CTC Trust. In each case, there is (and has been) a responsibility on the part of the school to assure sponsors that the funding has been spent wisely.

Conclusions

There are certain provisos to the successful introduction of new technology into the languages classroom:

1. Technology should be seen as the servant of the curriculum, rather than its master, and its place in the curriculum as a response to the learners' interest and needs.

   Technology has much to offer language learners and teachers. But the advent of a wealth of new multimedia technologies can distract attention from the true role of technology, which is to support and enhance the learning process. Technology is simply a powerful resource that should be harnessed to meet curriculum needs and achieve specific learning aims. The intention in this book is to demonstrate how a limited range of different technologies have been developed in different schools and are integrated into the curriculum;

2. Its successful implementation needs certain pre-conditions: senior management support, a whole-school approach, technology-literate teachers, technician support, a designated language learning accommodation (with particular facilities such as sound proofing) and a budget for staff training, materials development and the purchase of good-quality course material.

In brief, the use of technology in language learning will, if used wisely, greatly enhance language learning. To this end, the following seven points provide helpful guidelines:

1. Technology, on its own, is not enough to improve language learning; there are many other variables involved (see 3 below);

2. 'Hi-tech' equipment is no substitute for good learning tasks, course content and enthusiastic teaching;

3. It is fruitless to invest in integrated technologies until staff and students can handle the basics, e.g. effective learning from video and audio tapes, or using simple computer programs;

4. Choice of hardware, software and the language centre's design and layout should be driven by curriculum imperatives;

5. Many advertised multimedia language learning programs are designed for business people, are not truly 'interactive' (because they are read-only) and cannot be put across a network for multiple users;

6. There are pre-conditions to the successful introduction of technology into schools: staff training in relevant theory and practice, technician support, timetabled time for materials development and accommodation with certain furnishing;

7. The future technology for language centres is likely to be digital, rather than analogue.

The rapid fall in the price of hardware, the increasing interest in self-access language learning amongst the general public, the IT requirements of the National Curriculum, the increasingly computer-literate young people and the growth in international electronic communications will all ensure that technology, whatever its form, will have an increasing role to play in language learning.

I Flexible learning in modern languages

Lynne Kay, George Stephenson Community High School

Flexible learning was introduced into the modern foreign languages curriculum at George Stephenson Community High School over three years ago. Since then interest in, and commitment to, flexible learning methods has been growing not only in the department but in the school as a whole. It is seen as an enriching experience for both staff and students and the advent of the National Curriculum has strengthened the process. It is our view that the National Curriculum can be implemented successfully through a managed framework of flexible learning, which provides a better chance of tuning in to individual differences. Our approach has been to allow flexible learning to evolve out of the curriculum whereby the underlying principles and methods gain the commitment of staff and students over a period of time. The technological resources have grown too, but remain subservient to curriculum needs.

These ideas are neither new nor original. They support and build on good practice achieved through GOML, GCSE, TVEI and other developments. The George Stephenson flexible learning model is, however, one which has evolved in an LEA-controlled comprehensive with limited resources.

Flexible learning

In a flexible learning model, students are actively involved in a programme of work which is appropriate to their individual needs; they are working at their own level and pace, using a variety of resources and skills, including IT and other technologies. A crucial element is involvement in meaningful real life tasks, problem-solving and decision-making. This implies increased responsibility for the students. They can negotiate what to do, how to do it, why and when to do it, who can help and so on. They become involved in their own assessment and progress reviews and they design their own action plans, all within a framework of appropriate support.

This may seem daunting to those teachers who feel that the National Curriculum will remove flexibility, requiring more 'teaching to the test'. Some feel they do not have the necessary resources, or other ingredients such as an appropriate number of power points in the classroom, or adequate storage area, or even the 'right kind' of students. Some teachers feel genuine concern about those whom they feel cannot cope with responsibility, or who cannot be trusted to manage time or use resources effectively. It is feared that greater use of the target language may lead to greater disruption. These are genuine concerns which cannot be ignored.

Flexible learning does not, however, rule out effective whole-class teaching. It is more a question of balance and variety of activities, extending strengths, building on resources and providing support. Striking the right balance is crucial to motivation and the development of whole individuals.

The flexible learning approach was chosen and continues to grow in popularity for three reasons:

1. Flexible learning can offer a framework within which individual teachers can perform according to their strengths and gradually overcome fears and concerns through appropriate support;

2. There seems to be a greater awareness in all students of the resources available and increased accessibility both in and out of lesson time. Staff seem more confident using different resources;

3. It is compatible with the National Curriculum and meets the general aims for 'good' foreign language learning.

To be successful, flexible learning needs to satisfy the following four criteria:

1. Flexible learning has to enjoy high status within the school and be central to the School Development Plan. It will need a positive, mutually supportive, trusting environment, with the backing of Senior Management and the Head Teacher;

2. Suitable training for staff is needed. Just as a teacher might use different interpersonal skills, he or she will also have different management strategies and will need training and support in the use of new equipment;

3. Time and patience are needed when learning to use resources properly. A change in learning and teaching styles is needed. Developing communication skills, gaining competence and confidence to work independently or with others comes only gradually through interacting with peers, teachers and resources, and thus adequate support, trust and encouragement are needed. Some individuals cope better than others with increased responsibility. Some find negotiation and making choices quite overwhelming, but with support from peers and their tutor, all students should be able to work their way through their learning routes with increasing independence and confidence. Students will feel more involved, and less alienated, more inspired and less overwhelmed.

If students understand the purpose and value of what they are doing, then there is a better chance that the students will appreciate opportunities as early as possible and thus not abuse trust, responsibility and independence. For effective learning, the students need briefing on availability and accessibility of resources and increased awareness of the skills and strategies developed, as well as evaluation techniques. Support tutorials are essential. Students need regular teacher or tutor input. Tutorials provide a useful forum in which the tutor can provide feedback on the student's understanding and achievements, give praise and encouragement, impart knowledge and help students cope with difficulties, review progress and set targets.

Once inspired the students often feel motivated to extend their opportunities into private study and relevant homework, and wish to use the technologies in their own time e.g. lunchtime or after school hours, during extra support lessons;

4. Technological resources. George Stephenson Community High School has a whole school commitment to flexible learning and the role of IT. Our efforts have been supported and reinforced by Senior Management and initiatives within the school. Detailed planning, lengthy discussions, and elaborate structures for addressing Attainment Targets and Programmes of Study count for nothing without positive attitudes and a commitment to flexible learning approaches.

The flexible framework

Getting started and managing the process effectively will not happen overnight. There will be a lot of trial and error, and once in place, the flexible framework will need to be reviewed and developed continually. The guiding rules are:

- Do not be too ambitious to start with, try a small-scale trial;

- Identify carefully the initial group(s) to take part in the trial;

- Audit attitudes, methodologies and resources in the department
  - make the most of existing resources ;
  - decide what needs to be developed, adapted or purchased first in the light of National Curriculum needs;

- Let others know about initial development work – this could encourage support within the department and across the whole school.

As one of several methods, flexible learning has to be applied when and where appropriate to the learning objectives. In other words, it would be over-dogmatic to apply the flexible learning principle throughout the modern foreign languages curriculum regardless of circumstances.

Our modern languages department now runs a programme of flexible learning for every language learner across the whole ability range. The flexible programmes of work form about 50% of the learning process in Years 9, 10 and 11. This may vary at times according to the teacher, teaching group or individual need. The other 50% of time is used for whole class teaching where the teacher may make a greater input, presenting new material, and ensuring adequate coverage of GCSE topics, though still in a flexible working environment where a wide range of independent activities are encouraged. Obviously the students need to go through different stages before communicative competence is achieved. Flexible learning and the use of IT seem more conducive to practice and consolidation activities such as simulated communication.

The flexible programmes are designed at five levels covering Years 9 to 13. Each programme or route explains clearly the purpose and value of each activity. There are detailed instructions and references to a variety of resources, including but not restricted to IT. Each student follows a programme appropriate to his or her own level across a range of topics and experiences. It is thus possible for students to be working at different levels within the same classroom. Differentiation varies according to text, task, pace, guidance and outcome.

The flexible learning programmes of work have so far been used to encourage active participation of all students in the practice and development of discrete language skills: speaking, listening, reading and writing. However, as already suggested, evaluation and updating are a necessary part of the process. The department has begun to look at ways in which the flexible programmes can take into account multi-skill activities and cross-curricular assignments. Students are given a range of criteria on which to assess their own work or that of others. Work is reviewed periodically by themselves in negotiation with the teacher. Active discussions on criteria encourage greater critical analysis of strengths and weaknesses, provide more meaningful feedback and promote more effective action plans.

Classroom layout and accommodation

A resource base with adequate storage facilities is essential. We are fortunate to have our rooms along the same corridor. Two rooms are functionally equipped to provide a flexible learning environment. They are used as resource bases for both French and German materials. We often use the corridor as additional space for different aspects of independent work. Teachers' and students' old desks have come in very useful here. The next step is to furnish another two rooms as a specialist suite with specialist layout, furniture and display areas.

Room 16 (see Figure 1) is the main resource area in the department, with easy access for staff and students to share materials and use resources. The room is functionally specialised with listening booths at the back, and an adequate number of power points distributed around the room. This is conducive to individual, pair, and group listening.

Figure 1. *Classroom layout. George Stephenson Community High School*

The room has a built-in storage cupboard, in which tape recorders and headsets are stored. Audio and video tapes are kept in tape libraries. The tapes need to be stored and maintained in a highly organized way, otherwise this would lead to chaos and confusion. Tape stacks and extra shelving are useful for this purpose. It is also necessary to ensure adequate labelling and perhaps colour coding. In order to break courses down into smaller units or topic areas a larger number of shorter tapes of varying lengths is necessary. Technical support (e.g. audio-visual technician), a fast copier and a tape eraser are absolutely essential to the working of the suite. The video library is stored in the departmental office, which is also used as an oral studio to allow recording, editing, private viewing of videos etc. There is also a telephone in the office which connects with telephones in two other classrooms in the department.

With regard to furniture, the tables are usually placed around the periphery of the room as far as it is possible. This frees space in the middle for games and easy movement around the room. Grouping the tables facilitates group work as well as independent and pair activities. We also have a platform which is useful for role-play, performances, presentations and video recording.

As in each language classroom, there are four small white boards distributed around the room. This facilitates group work, presentation of notes, survey results, discussions etc. In addition to these small boards, there are two large white boards, which are useful for OHP activities. The OHP tends to be kept in the corner, as do the computer workstations, television, video recorder and the satellite; telephones are also around the periphery of the room. We try to use as little floor space as possible for shelves and units.

Selecting appropriate resources

Flexible learning can be packaged using different types of resources. There needs to be a balanced approach to integrating technology in a flexible learning model since the aim is effective learning, rather than using technology for its own sake. In the first instance, the aim is to make the most of existing resources and not necessarily to substantially increase stocks.

We use a range of materials (see below), because no one set of courseware is seen to be perfect or able to respond to all individual needs. The following four selection criteria are applied:

1. Suitability for self-study – vocabulary sections, support materials, answer sheets;

2. Coverage of and relevance to appropriate topics;

3. Interest value – length, subject matter, variety of exploitation;

4. Suitability for students' level of knowledge and skill.

Our resources consist of

- Home produced (paper-based) materials – using programmes of work, individualized routes, task sheets, role-play cards, answer sheets, review sheets, graded assessment tests, action plans;

- Commercial materials – books, readers and magazines, reference books, dictionaries;

- Software-based
    - CALL – dedicated software;
    - CBT (Computer-Based Training) – authoring software such as Databases, Word Processing, Desk Top Publishing, and so on;
    - IV (Interactive Video) – multimedia technology, combining sound, pictures and text;

- Audio and audio-visual
    - Interactive Video, Digital and Linear Video Technology, video from satellite;
    - Audio tapes;

- Telecommunications-based
    - Electronic mail, Fax;
    - Television - BBC, ITV, live satellite

Using learning technologies

Technological resources have been vital in providing a platform or context for the performance of productive communication in real-life tasks involving authentic contexts. Although there are many factors which help determine student perceptions, and thus uptake of modern languages, e.g. the Single European Market and the National Curriculum, the flexible learning model and the use of technology (IT in particular) have significantly raised the profile of languages. They have also improved student motivation and the way we address such issues as the European dimension, cross-curricular awareness, equal opportunities, personal and social development, economic and industrial understanding, cultural awareness and so on.

As students gain in confidence and become more familiar with the resources, IT and other technologies become allies in helping to maintain interest, motivation and alertness. Powers of retention seem to have improved through novelty and authenticity, challenge and fun. The students enjoy hands-on experience, learning by doing and interacting at their own pace, using realistic contexts. They enjoy problem-solving and reading for a purpose, using banks of information; producing written work seems more relevant, progressing gradually from narrative to discursive writing. Indeed, using technology as a springboard into oral activities can serve to make presentations, discussions and debates livelier and more dynamic.

Much of the software is used repeatedly throughout the range of levels. This ensures that elements of vocabulary or grammar are recycled for revision purposes. In order to help focus students' attention there is often a target involved. For example, they may have to time each other and keep a record of their scores. They must also make a note of any new language items encountered and learn them. Access is obviously important. Students must tick their names off on a sheet to indicate that they have had a turn on the computers, thus allowing the teacher to monitor who has been using the equipment and who has not.

The department is fortunate to have at its disposal a range of tools and learning technologies to develop flexible language learning criteria and thus enhance spoken language, particularly conversational skills. For example, we make regular use of our telephone systems, audio-video equipment, such as the video camera, interactive video and satellite television. Equipment is operated by pupils themselves, enabling them to work at their own pace.

A reading programme is also planned. Students are encouraged to keep a record or diary of what they have read. The listening and reading tasks are marked by the students themselves with the aid of marking schemes. Progress is monitored by the teacher, through regular discussions with the students, checking for feedback, scores attained, comments and opinions recorded and so on.

Before we could make effective use of our learning technologies, we needed to ask some preliminary questions, for example:

- What are we using them for? What is the aim? Is it for a specific teaching point, or more broadly to encourage student autonomy, differentiation, use of IT, etc.

- Who are they for? Are all students to have access or is one group to be selected initially?

- Are the resources easily integrated into the flexible learning framework?

- Is support needed? For students, for staff, or both? Is there a need to audit existing attitudes, methods and capabilities before setting up. For example, is an INSET day needed?

- How do we evaluate use and accessibility?

Using the computer

The computer has held pride of place among the technologies. Soon, being computer literate will be as important as knowing the three 'R's. Based on classroom observation, IT seems to contribute significantly to language learning and is conducive to good teaching. For example, it is patient and responds to individual needs, is consistent in terms of delivery, quality, instructions, guidance and response, it saves time, covering the same amount of material to the same standard, and it provides immediate feedback.

Independence, accuracy, range and complexity can be encouraged through use of software, ranging from pre-communicative word processing e.g. unscrambling, filling in gaps, moving text and editing, to producing free, independent communicative writing e.g. using desk top publishing or telecommunications. Interplay of criteria can also be encouraged through Interactive Video Technology, e.g. IV CD-ROM, IV digital, IV linear video, satellite and teleconferencing.

Rather than passively view what is on a linear video, the use of interactive video multimedia technology brings alive text-based resources by combining video, photographs, graphics and sound on a simple platform. It provides an effective, powerful means of presenting material, stimulating students' understanding and ability to respond, addressing all of the attainment targets, creating a 'real life' atmosphere in which to cater for different areas of experience. Students can be encouraged to interact with it and feel actively involved, thus gaining control over content and pace, and feeling more responsible for their own learning.

Using multimedia authorware

The department is looking at ways of properly integrating the authoring software into our flexible learning programmes. Authoring software can play a major role in relieving teachers of the mechanical side of marking, introducing a game-like element and supporting collaborative and independent learning. Students seem to appreciate the immediate feedback of a text manipulation program and enjoy the prospect of 'beating the machine'. If software adds a new and interactive dimension to language learning, it is likely to yield better results than when it simply replicates a paper and pen exercise.

Considerable time has been spent exploring authoring software e.g. *Trilogic* (developed in Poitiers) which allows us to tailor and exploit video material by editing, sequencing and superimposing text on the screen in the target language. Text can reflect content while not being a transcript. Another advantage is that less time is needed to wind and rewind since the frames have been numbered by the computer.

Utility Software and *PC Opensoft* have enabled us to experiment with *Siville* and *Louvre*, and some disks used in other areas of the curriculum. Students can access visual stimuli in a particular order and not just in the order in which they were recorded.

Siville is a French shopping simulation and as part of a small group of activities, has great potential. Native speakers in genuine surroundings react to your requests for directions around the town. On arriving at the shop of your choice, you go in, to be faced by a shopkeeper who asks you what you want and in what quantities. Your choices are indicated by use of the keyboard and are 'spoken'. The shopkeeper reacts to what you have requested and when you have finished, a display of a till indicates the amount you have spent in that shop. You can then wander off around the town to buy other items, or return to the woman at the beginning who will issue you with further instructions to buy certain items. Interacting in this way can obviously help students master intonation, accent and other skills. It can promote off screen discussions, role-plays, project work and debates, involving decision-making in authentic situations. Dedicated CALL software can also be used to complement the disk, e.g. Granville and its listening tasks using audio tapes, video and songs.

Using satellite and video

We have extended our video library to include not only a wide range of broadcasts from BBC and ITV, but also supported self-study materials downloaded and exploited from satellite television. Extensive research has been undertaken into the ways in which we can exploit news bulletins, soap operas, quiz programmes, documentaries, adverts and so on. The intention is to integrate these into the programmes of work at appropriate levels.

Used selectively and exploited at different levels, satellite television and video technology can be a valuable resource. As well as promoting European awareness, and developing insight into culture and civilization, it can be used as a springboard into other activities, thus integrating attainment targets, the different areas of experience and programmes of study. As well as promoting interest, enjoyment and competence at pre- and post-16 level, it can also serve to refresh and upgrade the teachers' skills and keep them up to date.

Effective use of satellite and video technology is very time consuming. Viewing in advance to assess the suitability and relevance of material, converting raw material into short, dense segments of teaching or learning material by differentiating tasks according to level of ability all take time.

For another view of using satellite technology at Brooke College, Corby, see Appendix E.

Using electronic mail

Following a successful bid for LINGUA funding to help finance VIth Form work experience in Angers and Poitiers, we benefited from exchanging information and sending messages abroad via electronic mail. This provided an interesting and authentic way of reinforcing existing links with the school in Poitiers.

However, despite its great potential, we did experience some problems: the telephone point has to be in an ideal place; it would have been preferable to use a machine next to the telephone point, permanently set up in a small room, and send messages over the network from one of the language classrooms, instead of from the computer room. Fax was also found to be cheaper and much simpler to use. However, our department will be involved in British Telecom's extension project to EDU 2000 1993 – exploring further uses of electronic mail with link schools in Europe.

Using Desk Top Publishing (DTP)

Word processing is perhaps the most widespread use of computers. With desk top publishing, however, it is possible to include drawings and pictures in text, and to produce a high-quality, professional finish. Some of our students have recently produced a French magazine using DTP. This included pages promoting the North East region, campaigns, various articles, reports, quizzes, questionnaires and survey results, promotional posters, adverts and so on.

We find that slower learners gain in confidence when they see the printout of their work from a DTP system. Writing for an audience can also lead to increased motivation and self-critical attitudes in students.

Overcoming practical obstacles to flexible learning

Curriculum planning

Time
Our Year 9 pupils have three 60 minute sessions: two French and one German. It is felt that 60 minute blocks of time are more conducive to practical work which encourages the development of a range of skills, and promotes problem-solving and technology-based learning.

Because it is felt that one contact per week for German is insufficient, we offer sessions during lunchtime and after school, thus optimizing access to resources and providing extra support and guidance. Demand for extra support sessions and clinics tends to be greater in Years 11 and 13, the final year for examination courses.

Audio-visual technician support
Valuable time can be saved by having a competent audio-visual technician, who helps to set up equipment, record broadcasts, prepare audio and video cassettes, labelling, keeping materials up to date and offering technical advice and support.

Teaching groups
The teaching groups were organized this year in bands, where sets 1, 2 and 3 were mixed and sets 4 and 5 mixed. However, we intend to introduce some setting whereby sets 1 will be taught separately from sets 2 and 3. It is intended that those students with special needs at the top end of the ability range will also be given special provision. Close liaison with our special needs co-ordinator is useful to ensure extra support in adapting and providing differentiated materials for the less able students.

Finance

George Stephenson High School has consistently sought finance from a range of sources to fund flexible learning and, as a result, has benefited from involvement in a number of projects on the leading edge of technology. At one level, the school has pursued a persistent policy of borrowing and sampling equipment from the major manufacturers before deciding to buy. At another level, it has pursued a proactive policy of entrepreneurship and has achieved funding from industry, government bodies and the European Community. We are currently bidding for TSI funding from the DfE. If we had not consistently sought funding in the past, it is unlikely we would have had the facilities to set up the flexible learning framework.

Industrial Sponsorship
This has been and will continue to be sought actively.

1. British Telecom plc has been a great ally in the provision of financial support for a number of projects initiated by the modern languages department;

2. The school has been chosen to be developed as a 'technological centre of excellence' by ICL. This means that a whole-school fibre-optic ethernet network with 486 servers and 386 PCs has been installed thus providing access to CD-ROM databases for all students and staff and opening up the opportunity to develop DVI training materials.

European Community Programmes

1. LINGUA enabled us to set up work experience for some of our VIth Form students in France;

2. PETRA and UBI have enabled us to set up teacher placements in Greece and Spain.

Government-sponsored agencies

1. SOBA is enabling us to explore possibilities in information transferrence via satellite;

2. TVEI enabled us to set up the early flexible learning structure;

3. The Central Bureau enabled us to undertake a joint curriculum project with geography and establish an exchange with a school in France, in order to promote environmental awareness in a European context.

Staff in-service training

With the use of more demanding strategies regarding interpersonal skills, managerial and organizational skills, greater demands are made on the teachers' own flexibility and he or she has to be prepared to develop a new role – that of facilitator, rather than sole imparter of knowledge. INSET has taken place at a number of levels both internally and externally and has been of vital importance when managing the process of change within the department.

Table 1. *The role of the flexible teacher*

Role	Tasks
negotiator/manager/guide	encourages/guides
designer of tasks/facilitator of learning	records achievement
assessor/monitor	keeps evidence,
	monitors performance and
	provides feedback

Staff have benefited from externally-provided INSET and have made efforts to share experiences gained from these courses. Most staff are confident using technology and are becoming more committed to developing their own IT capabilities, thus gaining experience as users of hardware and software. There now seems to be a greater understanding of the implications of flexible learning married to the National Curriculum (see Appendix D).

Example of planning a flexible learning lesson integrating technology: improving oral competence using the video camera and peer assessment

The stages in this process are:

1. Students prepare a dialogue

2. Following guide-lines from the teacher students are marked by one another on their ability to respond to individual questions with either 0,1, or 2 for each question. They are encouraged to feedback why they have given a particular mark.

3. At the next stage they think in terms of the PAIFIR criteria i.e. Pronunciation, Accuracy, Intonation, Fluency, Independence and Range. Clarification of what these criteria mean is always necessary. To begin with, peers will take it in turns, marking one criterion at a time for a number of students in turn. Again, students are encouraged to point out where mistakes have been made so that improvement is constant.

4. At the next stage, triangulation is used. One student asks questions, a second student answers and a third observes and takes notes according to the criteria. Feedback is essential if there is to be real progress.

5. Triangulation is maintained and groups film one another in turn in the oral studio (department office). Once filming is completed the cassette is brought back into the classroom and analysed using the criteria. Negotiation and whole group viewing will be necessary to sharpen up the students' ability to identify strengths and weaknesses.

The video camera has been used for improving spoken language in other ways too. In filming role plays, sketches, or a weather forecast, students had to analyse the result with a view to improving intonation, clarity, pronunciation, accuracy, and visual input.

Evaluation of flexible learning

Monitoring progress

Review is an ongoing process. Formal reviews take place twice a year when students discuss progress in some detail within tutor groups. Students back up their comments by writing down their feelings and thoughts and formalizing their action plans. On an informal level, the teacher may listen with a student or group of students. It may involve going through a piece of written work, offering feedback on oral performance, assisting with a computer program or finding out whether they like what they are doing, why or why not and so on.

The students themselves are responsible for monitoring much of their own progress (peer and self assessment) on a day-to-day basis; answer sheets and appropriate mark schemes are provided, and careful monitoring of this process is needed from the teacher to ensure that it is taking place. Progress is recorded through a matrix which gives details of the tasks to be covered in listening, reading, writing and using the computer. The teacher needs to ensure that enough time is being allocated to appropriate skill areas, and that quality of work and quality of experience are ensured. Teacher intervention, tutorials, and extra support take place as and when necessary.

With regard to Key Stage 3 and keeping evidence of students' work and a record of their attainment, we receive portfolios, i.e. a selection of students' work, from the middle schools. This mainly consists of samples of written work, and a profile of marks for other skill areas and teachers' comments. We obviously need to develop this in the future. For example, we intend to arrange for different types of oral work to be recorded onto tape (audio or video) and perhaps for a reading diary and listening record to be kept.

Subject take-up

The positive impact of technology on the languages curriculum is best seen by the increasing numbers of students taking up GCSE modern languages options (see Table 2).

Table 2. *GCSE figures*

Year of making option choice	No. in Year Gp	Girls Opting	Boys Opting	Total No Opting	Percentage
1988	202	43	12	55	27
1989	225	51	55	106	47
1990	210	67	47	114	54
1991	204	115	48	163	80
1992	195	70	86	156	80

The figures for 1992 reflect a dramatic improvement in the number of boys choosing to study languages. It is felt that as well as other factors such as the Single European Market and the National Curriculum, flexible learning methodologies, cross-curricular initiatives and the use of technology have helped raise the profile of languages.

Examination results and informal testing

We have also recognized the impact of our model on examination results. Our students are involved in end of unit assessment tests and end of year examinations. Although these tests do not form part of the flexible learning programme, it could be suggested that the latter has enhanced the language learning process in general, and thus served to enhance examination results. Indeed, success usually depends on thorough preparation and thorough practice through a variety of tasks and activities.

Each year we use the same mock examination papers for Years 10 and 11 and keep a record of results for comparison. Analysis at each stage, including final GCSE results, suggests an improvement in performance and higher levels of attainment. Above all, students enjoy using IT for language learning. This is apparent from the attitudes survey carried out as part of a regular monitoring and evaluation process (see Appendix F). Students are encouraged to express their feelings about what they are doing and how they are working.

The evaluation and monitoring in 1991/2 indicated higher levels of enjoyment, motivation and commitment. Progress in all of the language skills seems more rapid and levels of achievement, using the target language, also seem higher. The students work harder and appear more confident about what they are doing and understand why they are doing it. Whilst working through their differentiated programmes, the students are encouraged to achieve their own level in the different attainment targets, without falling behind or feeling left behind. Voluntary return for extra sessions after school hours and voluntary participation in a wide range of cross-curricular projects, including display work, are also indicators of higher motivation, commitment and more effective learning. But there is still a need for further progress and action plans.

Future action plans

1. Having explored extensive uses of satellite technology the main problem we see is finding time to make appropriate use of it e.g. advance viewing, editing, grading materials, and so on. We need to extend our video library and integrate satellite materials into the flexible programmes of work;

2. Due to involvement in the SOBA project and initiatives with Brooke College, Corby (see Appendix E), we are looking at how we can exploit technology to network with other institutions at student or staff level, for example via computer conferencing and satellite links;

3. We need to develop further our Interactive Video technology. For example, we need to extend our use of authoring software packages such as *Utility Software* and *PC Opensoft* for digital video, and *Trilogic* for linear video exploitation;

4. We need to integrate the use of a Concept Keyboard and ensure co-ordinated use of resources no longer immediately available in the department, but which are now centrally stored in a resources area in the

library. It is hoped that it will not be too difficult to ensure accessibility and flexible use;

5. We need to continue to adapt schemes of work in accordance with National Curriculum requirements at Key Stages 3 and 4;

6. With regard to areas of experience and the programmes of study, we need to develop work done through middle school and high school liaison, for example, ensuring adequate coverage of areas, adequate provision for differentiation, progression and continuity and special needs. We have already begun to design tasks at different levels of attainment, incorporating multi-skill tasks and agreeing assessment criteria.

Conclusion

Flexible learning is here to stay at George Stephenson High School. The aims and the structure of the National Curriculum can make a positive contribution towards more flexible ways of learning. Technology resources hold great potential and we hope that a steady growth in the development and use of these learning technologies will eventually bring down their prices and make them more accessible to a greater number of departments and schools. In our experience, coupled with a programme of staff support and a positive environment, they serve to make the language learning process more effective, more authentic and more meaningful.

II Upgrading the language laboratory to a multimedia centre

Bertold Weidmann, St.George's Grant Maintained Technology School, Sleaford

Modern languages and IT skills are given a high priority at St.George's School. Both are international in character and complement each other. The provisions for language teaching at St.George's School have been extended progressively over the last few years. The traditional pattern of French as the only language for most and then for all 11 to 16 year olds with only a few doing German as an option, was changed in 1991, when top sets in Years 8 and 9 were given an additional double lesson in German. In 1992, German and French became equal first languages in Year 7, Spanish was introduced as a second language in Year 8, and German was offered as a core and an option language in Years 10 and 11. In the near future, the current 'languages for all' policy will be extended to include the VIth Form.

Origins of the Brealey Languages Centre

The Brealey Languages Centre (BLC) opened officially as a purpose-built computerized languages building in 1985. It was the brain-child of local businessman Mr Reg Brealey, the school's Chairman of Governors. It was his intention to provide the pupils with the latest language learning technologies in an aesthetically pleasing environment conducive to group work as well as individual study.

Mr Brealey's two main objectives were to provide

1. A workplace in which pupils could study at their own pace whilst being immersed in the target language environment;

2. An opportunity for pupils to interact and co-operate with peers and the teacher.

At the beginning of the 1980s, this concept seemed to be achieved best by installing a language laboratory, combined with educational computer technology, which was then just emerging. Mr Brealey's aims, however, went further than to provide just the enabling technology: he wanted to create an appropriate environment for it and its intended use.

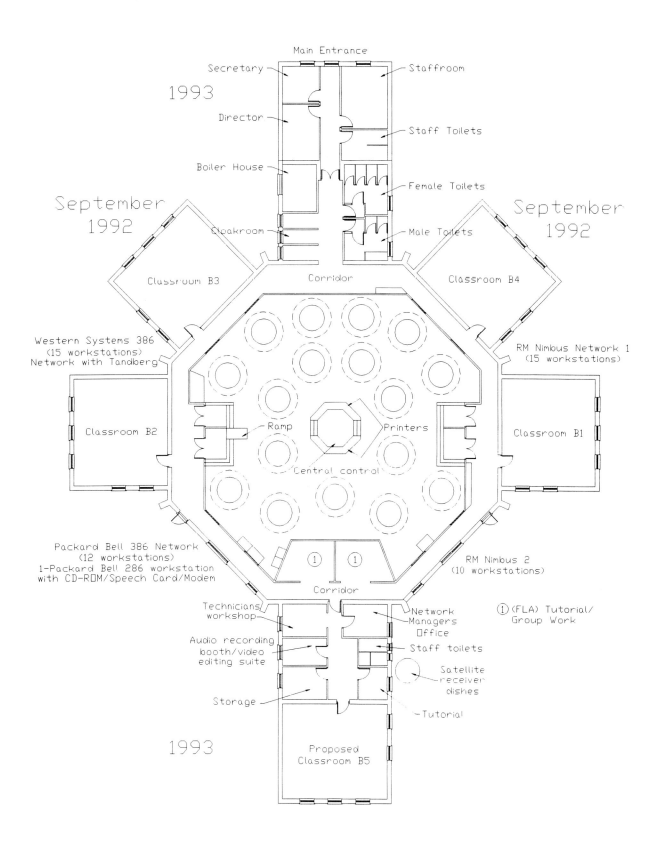

Figure 2. *Plan of the Brealey Languages Centre*

Planning and layout

After consultation with several prominent experts in the field of educational technology, the BLC was constructed as an octagonal building with an open-plan central area large enough to accommodate four teaching groups. Situated in the middle of the Centre is the teachers' control stand, octagonal like the Centre itself and slightly raised above the floor to provide an overview of the pupils' work areas. Grouped around the central console are 17 round work-tables known as 'mushrooms'. They have one central support and a raised middle platform for VDUs. Each mushroom incorporates three workstations, each of which can be shared by up to three pupils. As all cables connecting the mushrooms are under the suspended floor, the pupils' work area is free from obstructions.

A particularly striking feature of the building is its copper roof, rising high in the centre to end in an eight-spurred crown. This roof is supported on the inside by a spectacular, sound absorbing wooden ceiling construction which, free-bearing, starts on the walls and ends high above the floor under the roof-crown. On top of the teachers' console, hidden from view, are powerful lights which, together with spotlights round the perimeter, illuminate the whole of the Centre indirectly.

Access to the Centre is via an entrance lobby; from here a corridor rings the inner centre leading to classrooms and the office area. Initially, the BLC had only two classrooms which were on diagonally opposite sides allowing pupils to 'float' in and out of the Centre. In 1992, two further classrooms were added; a fifth classroom is planned for 1993. All the classrooms are well equipped with audio-visual aids and two are connected to the computing services available in the Centre.

The proximity of classrooms, the open-plan technology resource area, the high specification of the equipment, the dimensions and architectural features of the building and the special arrangements of the interior layout all contribute to creating a unique atmosphere and learning and teaching environment. The Centre appears airy and vast with its high ceiling, it eases team-teaching, it facilitates group work, it encourages partner consultation around mushrooms – yet it is quiet enough for individual study.

Technological specification of the Centre

Initially, the BLC was equipped with combinations of hardware systems deemed most suited for modern languages: computing, video and language laboratory facilities, supported by additional resources. Since then, whilst the computing and language laboratory facilities have been developed and expanded, the video technology has lagged behind, largely because the original tape-based system proved unsuccessful.

The audio section

The 30 workstations in the northern half of the Centre have always been part of a Tandberg Language Laboratory. Two master consoles are available, each servicing 15 workstations. However, just as the computer networks are bridged, so too are the two language laboratories: teachers can allocate different combinations of workstations to each master console and thus cater for small and large groups of pupils alike. Although the Tandberg cassette recorders have an interface to connect them to a computer, no attempts have been made to use it. At present, the language laboratory equipment still operates independently, technically speaking, although listening tasks form an integral part of many computer-based exercises.

The original computer specification

The original computers in the Centre were BBC Model Bs (and later on, BBC Compacts) and RM-Nimbus-186 machines. These were arranged in four networks: three BBC and one Nimbus network. The BBC networks were 'bridged' for greater flexibility. Networking computers has proved so successful both for teaching and for maintaining the systems that it is still a feature of the Centre today, though the original computers have long since been replaced.

Four major factors – two national, one European and one internal – have influenced the development of the BLC over the last couple of years and will continue to do so in the foreseeable future:

1. The Technical Vocational Education Initiative (TVEI), which prompted schools to look beyond the school gate;

2. The National Curriculum, which has changed our perception of the role of computers in school – and of their use in modern languages;

3. The growing importance of modern languages skills for all in the Single European Market which has enhanced the status, relevance and popularity of languages;

4. St.George's School becoming a Technology School.

All four factors have contributed to the decision to gradually up-grade the computing facilities in the BLC from the original mixture of educational computers to international industry-standard hardware and software.

Upgrading to IBM PCs

In the recent past, the BLC – and subsequently other departments within the school – have bought IBM-compatible 386 PCs with *Windows* and *MS-Works* as core packages, supplemented by subject-specific software as required.

At the beginning of the academic year 1992/93, the BLC housed a Novell-network of 30 PC 386 computers with two fileservers, a 10-station Nimbus-286 network with *MS-Works*, and a 15-station Nimbus-186 network.

Audio support for PCs

In order to provide audio support for 15 new PC computers, it was decided not to expand the traditional language laboratory facilities but instead to fit them with Tandberg voice cards. Two headsets (initially without microphone) are available at each computer for pupils to listen to recordings stored on the local hard disk in digitized form. At present, pupils can call up recordings within *MS-Works* (DOS-version) for word processing, spreadsheet and database tasks, and they can see French exchange pupils and listen to them in a presentation created with *IBM-Linkway*; in addition, software developed in-house will soon allow teachers to write their own language exercises and tutorials incorporating sound recordings. In all programs, the voice card is activated via the mouse by clicking on an icon or by selecting a speech file (see Figure 3). Although pupils were initially surprised to find 'talking computers', they quickly mastered the concept.

Both the voice card-based and the cassette-based audio support systems deliver high quality playbacks but – apart from technical considerations – each has advantages and disadvantages. The first can be integrated fully into the software and quickly locates and plays the required sound, but the pupils have no interactive contact with the teacher. Cassette systems are portable, i.e. the pupil can take the cassette away to listen to it at home or in a classroom, but on a long tape a beginner can lose her or his way trying to find the relevant information.

With the software we have, our impression so far is that the voice cards are better suited for self-contained computer-based flexible learning and self-study materials, while the language laboratories are more for teacher -guided sessions and school or home study material.

Although the quality and quantity of the hardware and audio provisions are very important, it is the software and its imaginative use by the teachers

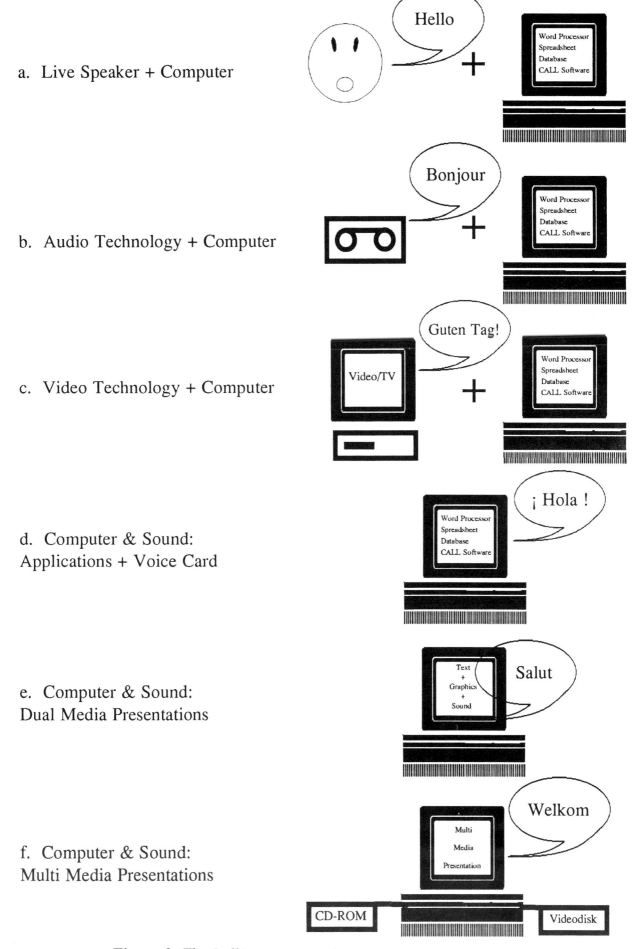

a. Live Speaker + Computer

b. Audio Technology + Computer

c. Video Technology + Computer

d. Computer & Sound:
Applications + Voice Card

e. Computer & Sound:
Dual Media Presentations

f. Computer & Sound:
Multi Media Presentations

Figure 3. *The 'talking computer'*

that brings the new systems alive for the pupils, and which highlights the constraints and limitations imposed upon them by older technologies.

Learning applications

Word processing, spreadsheets and databases play an increasingly important part in the languages work in the Centre: they are used by pupils, for example, to express their ideas in words and to collect, sort or find information – all presented in the target language. In preparation for independent work, teachers use them as 'authoring packages' to develop all four skill areas, by creating support material for classroom and 'starter documents' for computer sessions.

Introductory exercises concentrate on one skill and one application at a time, but pupils soon find themselves facing tasks which they can only carry out successfully if they use all four skills and a combination of software applications. One such example is written for the GCSE topic 'Accommodation'. In a simulation, pupils work as a receptionist in a hotel: their computer holds a database of guests (current and past), the spreadsheet presents a booking-in and billing form (see Figure 4), the word processor offers templates for correspondence, and the audio system records telephone messages. There might also be some handwritten letters. The pupils' work to deal with all inquiries consists of a series of tasks all involving a combination of IT and languages skills: starting with listening or reading to identify the problem, the process ends with writing or speaking to convey an outcome or result.

Whenever possible, teachers are encouraged to create multi-skill, mixed-application 'believable' situations. These integrated exercises allow pupils not only to practise and develop their language skills but also to work for their attainment targets in IT.

Software specification

The Centre, and subsequently the whole school, has standardized on *MS-Works*, first in its DOS version, then as *Works-for-Windows*. As an integrated package, *Works* has the advantage that data can be transferred from one application to another easily. Unfortunately, the Centre has only copies of the English version of *Works*, high costs prevent the purchase of the much-needed French, German and Spanish versions which would allow pupils to spell-check their work and use the thesaurus for vocabulary enrichment. We are currently seeking a 'Euro-edition' of *Works* (and *Windows*) with multilingual screen displays and dictionaries, or at least the option to buy in extra languages.

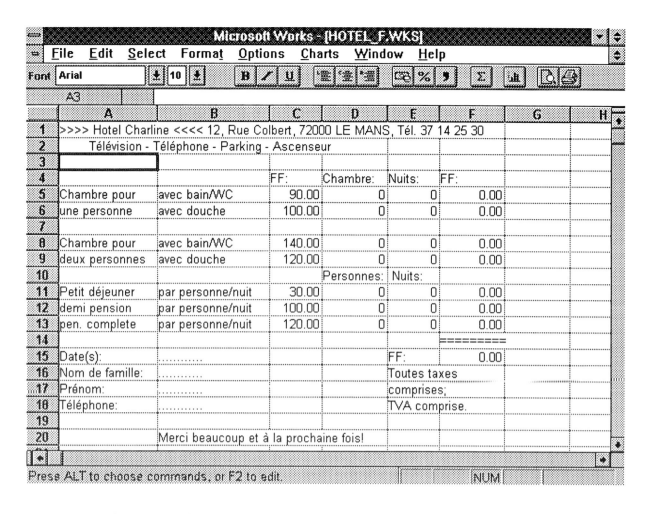

Figure 4. *Spreadsheet forms from Hotel Charline*

We have a range of 'tried and trusted' CALL software which is at present on the Nimbus networks. Increasingly, CALL programs are now becoming available for PCs. However, we are reluctant to buy CALL software which is just a version of the original BBC program and does not exploit the enhanced power of the new computers. There are, however, packages like *Granville* and *FUN WITH TEXTS*, which have been rewritten for the PC.

Internally, the department has to strike a balance between general applications packages and dedicated CALL programs. With new courses starting and with new hardware and software platforms to work on, the IT elements for all departmental schemes of work and programmes of study will take considerable time to develop.

Windows

Having decided on IBM-compatibles as the new hardware base for the Centre, *Windows* was the obvious choice for the operating environment: it is used in the 'real' world, it is international, it is mouse controlled, it is 'user-friendly' yet powerful, it can be customized and, once familiar with its handling principles, users can easily progress to other *Windows* applications. In the Centre, the potential power of *Windows* is restricted by the controlling network software which limits pupils' access and rights. In addition, one of the network log-in procedures resets *Windows* in all workstations to options imposed by the teachers.

Windows comes with a number of utilities and applications grouped under 'accessories'. The most useful of these at present is the art and graphics program *Paintbrush*: users can design their own images or manipulate ready-made pictures (clip art) and use them to illustrate documents created in other packages, such as word processing and desk-top-publishing. Teachers can also prepare illustrations which pupils have to alter (cut and paste), colour in or manipulate in other ways according to information they hear or read. Weather maps, town plans, and descriptions of rooms and people are just some examples of *Paintbrush* applications.

Desk top publishing

Page-Plus, which runs under *Windows*, was bought for 15 network stations and the staff computer in the office area. At present, modern languages staff use it mainly to create support materials, attractively designed and illustrated copy masters, classroom signs, posters, displays, and such like. The clip art supplied with the package was supplemented by the *Alde Spectrum Clip Art* CD-ROM and free clip art collections from bulletin boards. Additional material can be scanned in on an A4 grey-scale flatbed scanner.

FLIP

MS-Works lets a teacher write applications for their pupils but it cannot check or mark pupils' work nor highlight any mistakes they might have made, this is all left for the teacher to do after the lessons. In an attempt to provide learners with immediate feedback, and to ease the follow-up work of computer sessions for teachers, the Centre is currently developing FLIP, a Flexible Language Instruction Program. It is an authoring package offering initially cloze and sorting routines, and question and answer matching; other routines are to be added later. FLIP is specially written to utilize the Tandberg voice card and provide guided audio support. Built into the program is a monitoring option which records a pupil's achievements whenever he or she uses a FLIP tutorial and thus builds up a personal profile over a length of time. A separate program allows teachers to view and print out pupils' record files. Apart from use in lesson time, FLIP will also be used to start a library of self-access language material.

Additional software resources

Additional languages software on the PC network includes *Thinksheet* (in four languages), *Pen-Friend* and *Tick-Tack*. Network utilities are also used for modern languages, especially *Pegasus-Mail*, a freeware program, and *Chat!*. Both are great favourites with pupils who are allowed to use them for private communication in their spare time.

Support technologies

Satellite television

The BLC has two fixed-mounted satellite television dishes which allow teachers to receive broadcasts from two different satellites simultaneously. The receivers and recording facilities are located in the technician's workshop but the signal can be routed into the two original classrooms. While this arrangement facilitates the recording of broadcasts, it makes it awkward for teachers to utilize satellite broadcasts live in the classroom as they cannot change settings, such as channels, without leaving the classroom.

CD-ROM

The BLC has two CD-ROM drives, one attached to a computer in the Centre for use by pupils, the other in the office area for staff use. So far, languages and DTP CD-ROMs have not been used with pupils in Key Stages 3 and 4, but 'A' level students are encouraged to consult the multilingual dictionary and French encyclopaedia CD-ROM. As part of the network development, pupils will be able to address the CD-ROMs from any workstation.

Telecommunications

The BLC has a telephone line dedicated to telecommunications with sockets in the Centre itself and in one classroom. The diversification and expansion of the languages provision has increased the demands on all computer-based resources. At the same time, the role of tele-communications has changed from a support service to becoming an integral part of the IT developments for modern languages. E-mail is available internally on the PC-networks, externally through *CAMPUS 2000*. Electronic links enable pupils right from the start to apply and develop their newly acquired language skills by communicating with native speakers. Our partner school in Germany is also on *CAMPUS* and operates the same computing equipment and uses the same software (*Windows* and *MS-Works*) as we do; having this common hardware and software platform will greatly increase the possibilities and range of electronic exchanges between the pupils and staff of the two schools. The significance attached to telecommunications by the school is reflected in a special allowance awarded to a modern languages teacher to take responsibility for it across the curriculum.

Use and evaluation

Although other subject-users are allowed into the Centre, modern language classes are given preference. Pupils are allocated places in the Centre for half of their weekly language lessons in addition to having a base classroom. The booking system for the Centre is flexible. It is up to the individual teachers to decide when to take their class into the Centre and for what purpose. Currently the computers are not used to teach pupils new language material but to reinforce and practise material introduced in the classroom. Having prepared pupils linguistically and briefed them about their tasks in the classroom, the teacher takes his or her pupils to the Centre, where they work independently or in pairs. The teacher monitors pupils' progress and gives individual attention where necessary, either from the language laboratory master console or by going round from mushroom to mushroom. A well-structured session in the Centre, during which pupils work on a series of related tasks can also provide an opportunity for the teacher to deliver what the computer cannot do: one-to-one conversation and intensive oral work.

Our experience shows that pupils clearly enjoy working in the pleasant environment the BLC has to offer; this is reflected in increased motivation and willingness to work, even during lunch-times! New technology does not impede pupils' learning – on the contrary, most pupils quickly master the hardware and software available and benefit from it. Although we have no concrete evidence to support our claim, we believe that the individual work carried out in the Centre helps teachers to stretch each pupil to reach his or her potential. To cater for full differentiation, however, a wide range of carefully graded tasks needs to be available, a demanding undertaking best tackled by a departmental team and planned over a longer period of time. Using IT to such an extent contributes to the teachers' own personal and professional development.

On the practical side, staff using the Centre must be confident about using the equipment themselves and be able to explain it (even in the target language) to others, set a good example, and be willing to keep pace with technological developments. Most importantly, they must be prepared to create more and more teaching materials, structure their sessions well, adopt appropriate teaching methods and constantly develop them further. Without proper lesson planning, there is a danger that computer sessions deteriorate into time-wasting 'electronic baby sitting'. Whilst the Centre offers great benefits, it also makes challenging demands on pupils and staff alike.

On the management side, the new hardware and software, especially the networking equipment, makes great demands and at times expert knowledge is essential to make the systems as user-friendly as possible. Routine maintenence helps to prevent breakdowns, regular back-ups are essential, and a virus-checker is vital in an open system.

Future developments

The school's curriculum initiatives, coupled with the implementation of the National Curriculum will largely determine developments over the next few years. As regards IT, hardware and software provisions will need to be co-ordinated further in order to ensure that pupils can transfer and develop their IT skills, not only within the Centre, but across the whole school. Interdepartmental awareness and co-operation will be essential to achieve this, and the modern languages department as a major IT user will make a significant contribution to it.

In terms of equipment, the BLC hopes to

1. Provide *Windows* and *MS-Works* as the core software base across the whole of the Centre;

2. Add audio support to the one computer network without it.

The languages department will continue to review and expand the range of PC-based teaching materials, both for general applications and CALL packages. At the same time, the department will develop language tutorials based on *IBM-Linkway* and FLIP which will allow staff to work towards a multimedia environment. Continuous staff training, addressing both technology and methodology, will be needed to support all these developments.

III Developing an integrated multimedia approach to language learning

Paul Regan, Djanogly CTC

Technology as an enhancer of learning

The Communications Centre at Djanogly City Technology College, Nottingham, is a purpose-built electronic language learning centre which opened in 1989. It has been designed for school (11 to 18), community and business use, occupies the space of three classrooms and houses a 15-terminal (up to 24) IBM-compatible computer network with video and CD-ROM distribution facility, a 48-booth Tandberg IS10 audio-active-comparative language laboratory with TECS (a system which allows the teacher to control and view students' screens and to talk with them via microphones), and an interpreting suite.

In such a technology-rich environment, however, there is the obvious temptation to put the technology before the student and make inaccurate assumptions about the links between the learning process and the use of the technology underpinning it. During the evolution of the Centre the guiding objective in the use of technology has been the enhancement of the language learning process, which has informed both the direction of the curriculum in the school and, in turn, guided purchasing decisions on hardware and software, as well as giving direction to in-service teacher training.

That technology can enhance learning is a cornerstone of the underlying philosophy of the College and teachers therefore tend to accept certain assumptions about the multimedia method of language learning, namely, that technology can

1. Liberate the user from the most mundane tasks, and free him or her to be more creative;

2. Give a greater degree of control and personal autonomy to the student;

3. Lead to a high level of co-operation and team work;

4. Speed up a task;

5. Deepen and enhance students' understanding of the task.

These basic imperatives of technology can be built into the curriculum so as to enhance task-based learning by:

1. Placing students at the centre of the task, requiring them to initiate responses, to create their own programme, and to take or share responsibility for assessment;

2. Opening up whole areas of research through electronic mail and CD-ROM and giving students a rapid response to their own questions and prompting them to ask fresh ones;

3. Enabling students to produce a finished product which is well organized and presented, and encouraging professional execution;

4. Deepening the sense of worth of a task, i.e. using problems rooted in the real world, and through active learning. Used properly, the slow and often sterile process of language learning can be transformed into an exciting authentic task.

All these are generic attributes, rooted in learning generally. However, use of the word 'task' implies work of a more purpose-driven, integrated nature. In fact, task-based learning applies at Djanogly CTC from Year 7 and is related to problem-solving and getting results. Let us take, for example, the way in which the elementary traditional exercise of giving and receiving personal details can be transformed into a more demanding, integrated-skills task through technology.

The usual method (and still most commonly used) is to teach personal details by oral–aural question and answer routines with frequent repetition through pairwork. After a while this can become rather stilted and boring, since the number of partners and class-based contexts are limited. So can technology enhance personal identification routines, whilst satisfying, at the same time, the requirements of the National Curriculum for the use of technology and preferably with an integrated skills approach? One alternative model practised in the Centre has been to break the task down into a series of steps, each incorporating the use of various media at every turn, yet having as by-products the development of important additional skills:

Stage 1. Following the traditional teacher-led presentation stage, students watch a video of German children talking about themselves (NB later on they will be able to have control of the video by themselves at their own station);

Stage 2. Students practise the set phrases orally in pairs and groups;

Stage 3. Students are then given a brief explanation of some German letters, and written alphabet conventions by *Textreader*;

Stage 4. Students are taken through a word-processing software package in German by the teacher using a TECS system, explaining where the unusual German letters of the alphabet can be found on the keyboard;

Stage 5. Students are then requested to type in some of their own personal details in German and to get a print out;

Stage 6. They listen to a tape of German children and are asked to complete a number of exercises at their own speed based on this;

Stage 7. Students then send their details via electronic mail to their twin school in Germany (for further consolidation work later).

All these stages would be achieved in a double period. The obvious advantage of the use of media is that student participation is very high and active learning paramount. Also, by focusing on different media, the student has developed various skills: listening (to authentic peer speech), reading, letter-writing and handling electronic communications. The task has the purpose of linking up to a German exchange school where the information prepared will have a real purpose. The media have authenticated the task and, in turn, added credibility to the environment for language learning. The students have been freed from the repeated demands of the teacher and created their own challenges.

Prerequisites to the multimedia methodology

Language teaching technology will not provide a panacea for curing the problems of a poor or mediocre language department. It can never replace good teachers, thorough preparation, and wise management of students. If none of these three things are in place, then no amount of technology will work. Also, most students respond well to the challenge of technology but some do not. In other words, a new set of problems and priorities will arise for the teacher in terms of supervision and teaching style. So the use of technology will mean changes to methodology, learning styles and assessment practices.

There is nothing better than a fair balance, and the new skills which students will acquire should not replace, but complement, the language skills and knowledge which are equally important. It is difficult to achieve this balance, and it may take teacher and student several years to acquire what I would call a new culture of language learning. Once this has been achieved, however, it is easy for the teacher to give a formal lesson, or a lecture if he or she wishes, but only as one of a range of strategies which will be considered normal. This kind of model is obviously resource-intensive, not only in terms of hardware and software, but also in staff preparation time and training. There are also pitfalls for students, some of which are:

1. The danger of overwhelming the less able students;

2. Over-emphasis on the skills needed to drive the technology, rather than on the linguistic learning objectives;

3. A lack of continuity between the language centre and the classroom;

4. Difficulty in monitoring student performance and achievement at each of the steps.

The last point is probably the most fundamental because it is at the heart of assessment of students in language teaching, whereas the other three are really matters for classroom management and teaching methodology, which may require specific staff INSET.

The implications of all this for the language teacher (and his or her training) are therefore significant for the following areas:

- class management;
- teaching methodology;
- student assessment;
- learning outcomes.

In terms of deciding the development of a language centre, no investment should be made in technology without a review of the possible impact of technology on each of these four areas and a commitment to revising methods of teaching and assessment.

The student–teacher relationship in multimedia language learning changes substantially. Learning in the Communications Centre is part of an active experiential process in which students can search and experiment with the language through various media and participate with the teacher in their own assessment. The modern language centre enables flexible grouping, communication across groups or within groups, and with the teacher, so that the appearance of isolation is illusory. The pupil may be involved in a great deal more personal communication than in the classroom. The student has to cope with mediation and integration and has to manipulate the four skills in a variety of contextual situations – acting as transactor, interviewee, translator, interpreter or interlocutor.

Assessment, too, has traditionally been a limiting and often sterile process based on the notion of norm-referencing, placing undue emphasis on individual failure. The person who can best make sense of this progress is the student with the guidance of the teacher. The student knows what he or she can do, and what he or she must still do to complete a task. Technology influences this process and helps the teacher and student to concentrate on specific outcomes and practical applications of the underpinning knowledge and understanding, shifting emphasis away from a narrow assessment of teacher-led exercises.

Planning and designing a Communications Centre

Planning the facilities, hardware and software resource and physical layout of a Communications Centre should always be preceded by curriculum specification and planning. Too often, the hardware purchase precedes the specification of the curriculum and audit of learner needs, leading to great frustration on the part of incoming staff who find that the purchasing decisions that preceded them have little to do with their vision of the curriculum.

In the case of Djanogly CTC, the setting up of the Centre involved many months of careful negotiations with school governors, business sponsors, manufacturers and suppliers. Indeed, any multimedia installation would need the same approach. The main priority was to achieve the most flexible layout in terms of usage and accommodation for the maximum possible number of students, i.e. an authentic and stimulating environment, and all this at the most reasonable cost.

The first obstacle to be overcome during the early stages of preparation for any newcomer to language centre development would be the design of the room and the amount of space allocated to the Centre. Much depends, of course, on planned future functionality. For, example, the Centre might incorporate IT teaching, and also be the base for audio-visual materials capture, preparation, maintenance and storage for the whole college.

Whatever happens, no purchase should go ahead without a total vision for the use of the Centre over at least a five year period. Some notable educational institutions have made the mistake of changing their minds about use of the Centre too late and been unable to make the necessary changes. An example of this would be where trunking needs for the design of the centre furniture took no account of the possible addition of IT workstations in the future. The designer should bear in mind, above all, that classrooms are not being lost but space gained since the creation of a third space from the conversion of another classroom would create an extra room for group work, or work away from the technology.

When furniture and layout have been provisionally agreed with regard to aesthetic and functional considerations, the premise for selection of equipment should be that it be advanced, modern and reliable. The seductive lure of cheaper equipment, or equipment with more gimmicks than efficiency, should be avoided as a false economy, and a poor platform for developing sound curriculum programmes. The entire system should be controlled by micro-processors so any future software developments can easily be included. Every conceivable function should be included as standard. It should be possible to control up to 100 student positions by a single ribbon data cable thus avoiding vast amounts of trunking in installation. The whole system should be linked up between the language laboratory, video and satellite systems. Link-up with IT and on-line facilities, TECS, and simultaneous translating systems, as well as provision for video editing, will turn a language laboratory into a multimedia Communications Centre.

Functionality

A well-equipped centre may be a technology show-piece but, more importantly, it is an area in which many languages can be taught effectively to different consumer groups: school children, business people, teachers and the local community. It is also an area which can be accessed by industry for everyday language services. These competing requirements mean that the Centre:

1. Must have the flexibility to accommodate a varied number of teaching groups working simultaneously on different language tasks, allowing for intra-group and inter-group communication;

2. Must provide back-up resources, on-line access, and computers linked to a network;

3. Should be located within a suite of rooms designated for language use, but

4. Should also be adaptable for multi-use (including non-language use);

5. Must be user-friendly, i.e. students should be aware of the total potential, and commercial users should be sufficiently impressed that it can tutor them and that it can be used commercially;

6. Should contain sufficient working and writing space for each individual;

7. Should allow easy transition between facilities;

8. Should enable rapid communication both within the group and outward to the world via e-mail and satellite television.

The basic operative hardware unit of the traditional language laboratory is the cassette recorder. In Djanogly CTC this has been enhanced to allow network recording, conferencing, grouping, conversation and interface with video and computer. As in the case above, interaction with the computer network allows the student to integrate use of all the language skills in a single task, or simply concentrate on any one: listening to a tape from a friend, word-processing a reply, printing it and sending it via electronic mail to a correspondent and receiving and processing a rapid reply.

Satellite link-up through a video network brings live or recorded television. A video camera installed in the teacher console can send round an image of a piece of text while the teacher discusses it with the group through the headphones.

Purchasing policy

This chapter has not mentioned specific manufacturers or suppliers, but any customer should be aware that hardware purchase is a minefield. Furthermore, what is right for one school may be wrong for another. However, there are some ground rules:

1. Before any purchases are made, have a fairly clear design for layout, and clear expectations of what you wish to achieve in terms of student response;

2. Any IT purchase which is made will probably be dependent on many other factors which do not bear on the Language Centre. Remember however to lay down provision for flexible use and addition at any later stage;

3. The technology is changing very fast. However, in my opinion, it will be several years before language teaching facilities make any kind of quantum leap and in the interim the very latest technology will be very expensive.

Learning objectives within the Communications Centre

The two fundamental learning objectives of a multimedia centre are to:

1. Provide a base for rapid access to information;

2. Provide students with the means to analyse, process and make decisions about how to act upon that information.

Accessing information

The teacher acts as a facilitator who empowers the student to access a wide spectrum of information. His or her job in this instance is to ensure that the material is relevant and that it is accessed correctly. The IT network gives ready access to, among others:

- CD-ROM: academic encyclopaedia; technical and education referencing; indexing and abstracting services; *NERIS*; *ECCTIS*; media information; interactive video;

- On-Line Access: e-mail; *CAMPUS 2000* (Educational); *Prestel*; banking; teleshopping; databases.

Handling and presenting information

The support service and teacher commitment required are quite substantial. For the development of learning materials, recorded satellite television programmes must be edited, their meanings and structures extracted and often presented through support materials alongside the video and audio.

Little more than 10% of two to three hours of unselected satellite material can be used directly in a class without any modification.

However, texts prepared by the teacher out of an information bank built up over time can be manipulated, edited, presented, cut and pasted and published in some form by the student. Letters can be composed and translated using programs such as *Tick-Tack* and *Pen-Friend*. Tapes can be enjoined with edited textual images or with computer programs such as *PC Globe*, or short clips of satellite material, such as Meteosat weather pictures or UOSAT space data. Software simulations such as *Into the Unkown* can bring history alive while back-up information can be provided on tape or screen. The final result will be the student's own work right down to publication. Ideas can then be developed on the word-processor and further research undertaken through on-line access and CD-ROM.

In brief, the student can work at his or her own pace, but can also be empowered to work rapidly; he or she can develop a number of intellectual, creative, language and personal skills. Moreover, the Centre can be used by students of English, modern languages, statistics, economics, humanities, IT, business studies, desk top publishing and mathematics.

A communications centre model at Djanogly CTC

Layout and hardware

The Communications Centre at Djanogly CTC is able to incorporate the facilities described above in a relatively confined space on an open-plan design based on three average classrooms and includes a simultaneous interpreting suite (see Figure 5).

Accommodation within a space about 11 metres by 15 metres comfortably provides for 48 pupil stations (2 classes of 24). However, this number can be increased to half as much again (72) with each mushroom section increasing from 4 to 6 stations. Small spaces for group study and seminar work are also needed.

The Centre is notionally divided into two teaching areas, with free access between the two halves. The language side contains 24 pupil stations linked to the console with networked and cassette recorders. Each station is enhanced by a video monitor also linked to the console.

The monitors can be used for three purposes:

1. To receive satellite television;

2. With VCR playback to allow student control of the video tape;

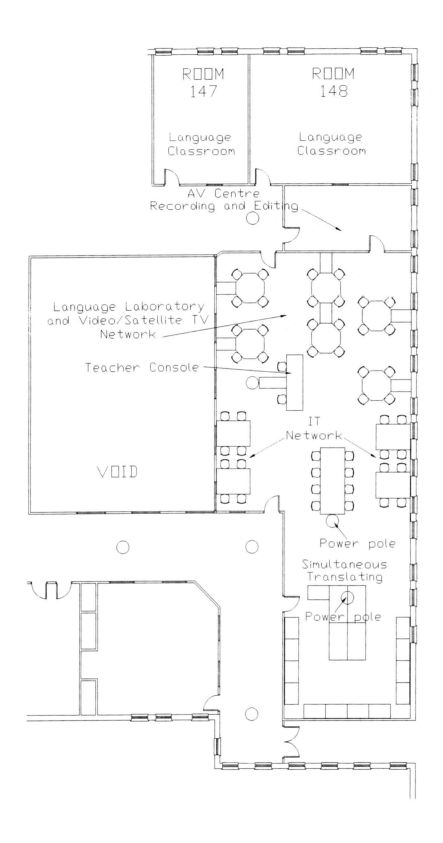

Figure 5. *Plan of the Communications Centre at Djanogly CTC*

3. To receive textual images from the teaching console.

As with audio tape control, the teacher can monitor each screen from the console, and communicate to the whole group, sub-groups or individuals.

The other half of the room also contains 24 audio cassettes plus a maximum of 24 networked computer screens. Remote and local printing attached to the network with continuous line-feed is in place. The installation of a TECS computer system based on the teacher console enables the teacher to have the same kind of contact with students at PC stations, with the ability to control screens, view screens, and to talk via microphones.

The whole room is controlled and monitored from a T-shaped teaching console, having two teacher stations. Each station has a master cassette function, video monitor and VCR. The console also carries a fixed video camera focussed on a working surface for text transmission.

Separated from the Centre by a partially glazed partition wall is an audio-visual centre. In addition to being a base for audio-visual equipment, this room houses the receiver for satellite television which is then transmitted into the Centre.

Furniture

The furniture requirement for all this is exceptional and the specification takes into account maximum use of space, user flexibility, need for durability and for appearance. It should in fact possess the three classic requirements of the architecture of the Ancient Greeks – venustas, firmitas, utilitas – beauty, strength and utility.

The central console is supported on six four-station mushroom octagonal tables, constructed of laminate used with metal supports. Four sides of the table house the cassette boxes, three sides are empty for extra use, and one side also forms the edge for a connecting oblong table. These oblong tables have three functions:

1. To provide extra working space;

2. To carry the trunking;

3. To house the VCRs on shelves.

The video monitors are placed on a circular surface raised above the table and are effectively just above eye level. It is important to note that the straight-edged octagonal tables are better than the more aesthetically tempting round tables because they give a wider and more secure working space for the student.

The IT facility is housed in six more traditionally designed benches of the same material. The benches provide room for monitors, disk-drives, keyboard, and TECS reception.

The floor of the Centre is carpeted to reduce noise and the walls J-tracked to allow for flexible display (i.e. moveable white boards running on wall-mounted tracks).

Conclusion

There is clearly a great deal to be gained from a decision to use technology for language teaching. Teachers become enablers, students take a more positive role in their own learning and assessment, and modern languages take an active place in the school curriculum as a part of the technology continuum with science at one end and business studies at the other. If schools were to start replicating real life tasks in language learning, then the skills learned by the students would carry them into their careers where knowledge of business and language skills for export sales and marketing and European awareness would all be useful assets. Business and enterprise skills are increasingly at the heart of our curriculum, and may help to turn the country's trade deficit around in the early years of the next century!

IV ELOQUENT: the LINGUA interactive digital language project at Thomas Telford School

Stephen Hagen, CTC Trust

ELOQUENT is a LINGUA-supported project running over 2½ years with the following complementary aims:

- The design and installation of a fully-digital self access, networkable multimedia language learning centre, based on the Archimedes A5000 platform and located at Thomas Telford School, Telford;

- The design of interactive learning materials in German, English, Greek and Italian for post-16 students, integrating audio, text, still pictures and motion video. The intention is to go beyond all the facilities of a traditional language laboratory by adding the value of multimedia applications operating in real time.

The rationale for the project

Multimedia – the way ahead?

Today's generation of young people have been reared on sophisticated pop videos and startlingly realistic computer graphics and many become quickly disenchanted with systems which do not have full-motion video, live broadcast material or impressive graphics.

Traditional text-based computer-assisted language learning (CALL) packages are far from fulfilling their promise of becoming the panacea language learning tool. Research on adult user needs indicates that people associate certain media with particular skills:

- Printed material for reading, writing letters and reading technical and sales literature;

- Audio for travelling abroad, and listening and speaking skills (good for practising pronunciation and listening to authentic dialogue);

- Video for travelling and listening to talks;

- 'Live' native speakers for practising telephone skills, 'wining and dining', listening to talks and customer meetings.

In this respect, four of the current language learning technologies on the market are seen as 'promising' by users (see below). The Training Agency Report (1990: 61) gauged the order and level of interest in each as:

1. satellite   (58%)

2. multimedia   (57%)

3. interactive video   (57%)

4. CD-ROM   (51%)

Adults and post-16 students rate interactive video and artificial intelligence (AI)-enhanced CALL as 'promising', but less so than the word processor, satellite television and multimedia. As far as can be stated from the figures, traditional CALL, interactive audio and fax are adjudged to have the poorest future prospects (Training Agency Report, 1990: 64). Good interactive language learning design integrates all of these technologies into a single, more powerful tool for language learning; any single technology applied alone is less effective than a combination of two or more.

Multimedia applications offer a rich language training environment and learning experience by combining interactive audio and video technologies with the computer. This enables the learner to interact with the system through any one, or several, of the media. The integration of the various media on networked or stand-alone workstations, however, presents possibilities for applications developments which are entirely new and challenging. This is why the development of multimedia technologies has been hailed as one of the most important IT developments for languages in recent years. One of the main attractions of new multimedia technology is the potential it has for fostering a communicative approach to language learning by utilising a wide range of stored information which directly reflects the real life and culture of the target language. Above all, there is the impact on the learning experience (NCET Report, 1991: 78).

In these applications, diverse sources such as newspapers, video footage, images of artworks, or radio broadcasts can all form the basis of a single coherent tutorial interaction. Multi-lingual dictionaries, reference materials and word-processing tools can be included for use in a wide variety of tutorial exercises; the potential for combining sound, pictures and the written word in multimedia applications makes this a very powerful technology. The possibility of sound recognition of commands, student repetition, recording and storage of digitised sound increases the potential for interactive language learning substantially. The learner would be able to work for longer periods without intervention by the tutor and vary the activity to maintain interest.

The main difficulty is how to exploit the available technologies in innovative ways in order to translate its potential into realizable end-user applications which are more effective than existing single media approaches. The deficiencies are the lack of available learning materials, the uncertainty over which technology to use and the high cost of IV materials development (for example, the design and production costs of a Laservision IV disc are approximately £100,000, including filming). On the other hand, companies using this form of language learning technology report that there are 'considerable savings of time' in this form of learning (NCET Report, 1991: 79).

However, since multimedia language learning is relatively new, little research has gone into the development of a learning model.

Design considerations

The optimal language learning environment does, however, introduce further variables when new technology is added. That technology can enhance language learning is an oft-made assumption without much substantiation from longitudinal studies. In seeking a technologically-rich learning environment, we should ask many questions including: What educational strategies and tactics which are appropriate for CALL can be related to the specific media that are available? What forms of interaction are appropriate to each one (between sound, graphics, text, paper and video)? What is the relationship between the different media, and what forms of adaptivity does each one facilitate? How is each user-group to be defined, and so on.

The area of CALL is still in its formative stage; there is little well-developed theory on which to base courseware design. Much previous work in CALL, both in courseware development and in the (rare) observation of learning, has concentrated on repetitive exercises in the 'drill and practice' style, often involving text-manipulation exercises like gap-filling, 'text-unjumbling', or vocabulary-learning exercises. This approach may be seen as a legacy of the programmed learning approach to education and training.

Most language teachers would agree that the way forward is to focus on the 'communicative approach', which emphasizes the students' involvement in, and interaction with, more realistic situations, and which places less emphasis on the learning of grammar rules, and more on developing communicative strategies in 'real situations'. Until they can learn to speak and respond intelligently, however, computers will always be treated with a healthy degree of scepticism by the language teaching fraternity.

Parallel to these developments in CALL, there have also been more general developments in computer assisted learning, leading to approaches which attempt to give the student more control over the interaction with the machine, and more choice in what and how is studied. Greater control is seen as producing greater motivation and engagement, and thus more effective learning. In particular, there is little empirically-based observation of how students learn a second language with a computer, i.e. which learning strategies they employ at different ages and stages of learning.

There are a number of issues arising from CALL which provide some guidelines: the system should be

- user-friendly and flexible;

- consistent in its design and specifications (for example consistent in the use of keys, commands and screen design);

- based on sound psychological and pedagogical principles from the realm of second language acquisition research.

Towards a flexible learning model

The ELOQUENT project has drawn heavily on second-language acquisition theory as the basis for its tentative learning model. In this respect, the work of Krashen (1981, 1985), Burt and Dulay (1977, 1978) and Stevick (1976) has proved useful.

To be effective, a language learning programme has to present the learner with digestible new material ('comprehensible input') which he or she finds relevant, interesting and abundant enough for different types of practice to be chosen. On the other hand, the learning material has to be graded or sequenced into different levels of difficulty.

Multimedia design for language learning can be based on the following four characteristics:

1. *Comprehensibility*
   The programme will supply comprehensible linguistic input; in other words, material that is presented can broken down into digestible pieces appropriate to the student's level;

2. *Interest/relevancy*
   The interest of the learner has to be retained by making the content vocationally relevant;

3. *Sufficiency of input*
   If the foreign language classroom should ideally be filled with comprehensible input (Krashen, 1981, p. 105), the program's capacity to provide an abundance of relevant material in various media (sound,

4. *Sequencing*

Grammatically-sequenced syllabi traditionally present the structure once, and other material is then subordinated to each of the structural learning points in turn. Here, the focus will be on function and skills development, where language is graded and grammatical explanation is separately provided on a hypercard. The student is then free to self-navigate, taking either the 'acquisition route' (unlimited exposure to material at various levels), or the 'conscious learning' path, i.e. following a guided learning route through the material.

Since the process by which people learn a second language is highly complex and remains largely unfathomable due to the large number of variables, the design of both the courseware and the tutor system can only follow hypotheses. However, since learning 'can, and usually does, involve deductive and inductive processes' (Higgins, 1988: 51), multimedia-based open learning should allow learners to engage in exploratory learning, but with an option on calling in structured exercises when they feel fit, thereby using both inductive and deductive learning styles.

The design of multimedia learning packages should incorporate certain features:

- Multiple entry points to allow students to by-pass uninteresting or known material;

- Tutorial support to help in understanding and difficult language areas;

- Alternative learning routes to enable learners to choose between situational, skill-based, function-based or grammar-based approaches to syllabus design.

The need for a totally flexible learning model to be incorporated into materials design begs the question of whether the technology can deliver.

The learning environment

Defining student needs

In functional terms, the student has to be able to access language training material which is interactive and carries sound, pictures and graphics. He or she should be able to access it in stand-alone or networked mode, and record his or her own voice samples into the program in answer to questions in the program. The student will need a system which will employ state of the art techniques in both hardware and software, but at the same time will allow the use of most IBM-compatible programs, including current language learning software in a cost-effective, student-initiated, student-directed learning world.

language learning software in a cost-effective, student-initiated, student-directed learning world.

The workstation or network is linked to a modem so that students can get on-line information from other systems such as CD-ROM, teletext and satellite, and can access and edit the material. The aim is for digital video editing of satellite broadcasts so that learning materials can be assembled more easily and fed into each workstation (copyright permitting!) as required either down a video channel in the network or by Genlocking the signal to the computer display.

In the networked version, samples are transferred across the network to a hard disk and filed ready for the student to access. The student can control samples by several methods: clicking on the screen with a mouse, using a touch screen, or ultimately by voice recognition. Each sample is labelled by the session and stage. Samples can be joined by the student or teacher by dragging two samples into a join icon. Pre-recorded samples which ask questions or deliver continuous text are stored on CD-ROM and can be manipulated by the student to carry out exercises, e.g. compose a letter (oral or written) or narrative. The sample can be processed so that intonation can be altered to convey varying messages, e.g. raising pitch. Each station has a directory linked to it with sub-directories allocated to individual system users, so files are automatically labelled and stored – ready for the tutor's evaluation or the student to return to later.

Checklist of learner needs (see also 'student recorder' in Appendix I):

Learners need a system which

- enables them to work and study at own pace and in own time;

- removes inhibition;

- encourages development of 'learn how to learn' strategies;

- improves motivation by putting learner in control of learning;

- provides mobility, learning at home or in workplace;

- guarantees authentic sound, rate and contextualisation of speech;

- allows visual access to socio-cultural clues to meaning e.g. 'body language';

- provides instantaneous response and renewal of models for repetition;

- enables student to focus on speaking, listening, reading, writing, individually and in any combination;

- provides in-built support;

- provides phrases with or without subtitles in optional languages;

- provides role models and pronouncing dictionary if required;

- enables learner to record and playback his or her own version to compare it with the model;

- enables learner to role play with others;

- contains tnumber, spelling and word processing options;

- provides access to native speakers.

In brief, learners need a system that allows them to work independently, more intensively and with greater concentration than in conventional language learning situations. The system can be used to replace much of the intensive phase of language learning, where the focus is on visual presentation of new language in context, back-up explanation, consolidation and practice. The advantages are authenticity of sound and sight, endless patience, the freedom of the student to roam at will through inter-related aspects of grammar, vocabulary and writing exercises.

Defining the tutor's role

The tutor in the multimedia language centre will want to be able to input the training program remotely on the student's network. The tutor may or may not be physically present in the classroom. In the case of remote monitoring, the tutor should be able to communicate messages to the student's workstation either as an audio broadcast, or by flashing a textual message across the screen (ideally by opening a window). Ideally, she or he will be able to interrupt the student's program, even close it down, in order to get immediate feedback from the student.

The tutor will need to correct the student's version either by re-running the student's program, stopping it or slowing it down, or by inputting his or her own model – possibly by dragging it into a window on his or her own (master) screen, so that it appears on the student's screen. The tutor should also be able to store the student's responses digitally for later evaluation.

Checklist of tutor requirements (see also 'console' in Appendix I)

The tutor's system should

- free him or her from routine (teaching by drilling and repetition, which can account for 40% to 50% of learning time);

- enable him or her to concentrate on more creative aspects: curriculum development, presentation, explanation and human-interface support stages;

- enable him or her to customize the package to suit the learner's or trainee's needs.

The tutor will, however, require training in interactive courseware development, since the additional freedom carries with it a new responsibility for innovative screen-based design.

Selecting the platform resources

Selecting hardware

In terms of selecting an inexpensive multimedia digital development platform for languages, the choice is currently between the following three systems:

- A *Windows 3.1* environment on an IBM-compatible 386sx or higher, either with a Soundblaster Pro stereo sampling and playback kit, possibly using *Authorware Star*, or a plug-in DVI board;

- *QuickTime* running on an Apple Macintosh II LC;

- *Replay* on the Archimedes A5000/A540 with RISCOS3.

Both *Replay* and *QuickTime* effectively place a video recorder inside the computer. This enables moving pictures, sound samples and colour stills to be stored in a database, e.g. on a CD-ROM, from where they can be cut and pasted like text into a language learning program. Each works with an authoring package; *Replay* with *GENESIS II*, *Magpie* or *Key Author* and *QuickTime* with *HyperCard*, *StoryMaker* or *Authorware Professional*. Both compress each image before it is stored, which allows many more pictures to be stored, but also leads to some loss of quality.

Replay and *QuickTime* have the advantage of running on existing classroom machines:

Replay: (Minimum system) A3000 with ARM2 processor and 2 mb of memory will play pictures at 12.5 frames a second. Machines with an ARM3 processor (A540, A5000, upgraded A440) will play pictures at 25 frames a second. An additional CD-ROM drive would, however, be necessary to access some *Replay* films.

QuickTime: This is designed for machines with a 68020 processor, or better. The minimum operating system would need to be 6.07, or more recent. It can be used on a Classic II with 2 mb of memory, but the pictures would be in black and white. Minimum spec: Apple Macintosh LC with 4 mb of RAM. To display 256 colours (a Video RAM [VRAM] upgrade would give more than 30,000 colours). A CD-ROM drive would be a necessary add-on. To record movies, an LC, digitizer card and video camera would also be needed.

Time and speed are also factors: e.g. a Macintosh LC will take five minutes to compress a one-minute movie, while low-end Archimedes machines can only display 12.5 frames per second, half the normal speed of television pictures. The effect is movements similar to those seen with a strobe light (although this is less obvious in a window) but will adversely affect language learning programs where 'lipsync' is vital. Machines with a higher specification, such as the A5000, can display the full 25 frames per second needed for full-motion video. The frame rate of Macintosh varies with the specification of the machine, though picture quality in both systems declines noticeably with full-screen pictures. *Quicktime* depends on which model of Macintosh is used: it can play as low as 3 or 4 frames per second on 16 bit machines, or as high as 30 frames per second on the new Quadra.

Multimedia authoring systems

Currently, there are three broad categories of system which could be used to develop multimedia language learning materials:

1. Frame-based systems
The traditional computer-based training system where a branching program presents frames of learning material in a sequence which is either fixed or conditional on specific student responses. *Authorware* and *Avanti* are examples of such systems.

2. AI systems
These utilise techniques from Artificial Intelligence (AI). They are frequently referred to as Intelligent Tutoring Systems (ITS) and usually attempt to diagnose an individual student's cognitive state and adapt their tutoring to it.

3. Hypertext or hypermedia systems
These present large quantities of learning material whose units are linked either hierarchically or associatively. The student may be free to explore these as they wish, or may have some structure imposed on their explorations. *HyperCard* and *Linkway* are examples of such systems.

The ELOQUENT software platform had to be chosen from among these types of system. The old-fashioned branching or 'frame-based' systems are generally seen as dull and de-motivating for students since they do not use the inherent power of computers to enliven study, and have a very limited set of responses to student input.

Given these considerations, a form of hypermedia would be an appropriate basis for the design, if a structure corresponding to the adopted curriculum were also to be defined within the environment. As the courseware design has developed, a software environment of sufficient power has been chosen, which will either provide or support the development of tools required to produce the multimedia interactivity that the design specifies. Specific materials appropriate to the courseware design, which satisfied the curriculum specification proved more difficult to obtain, largely due to copyright confusion over the use of moving video.

Sources of material

Ideally, the use of digitized, full-motion video and a hypermedia delivery system means that learners can enjoy the advantages of being instructed by native speakers 'on location' in real life situations while remaining in control of the pace of instruction, incorporating options on repetition and revision. The real tutor, if available, would be released from routine work, have more time to facilitate the learning, instantly monitor and correct the output, store the output digitally and provide human-interactive assistance in the active, oral aspects of the language. Selecting appropriate material or creating it from scratch is a critical step.

Audio
There is a vast range of audio material readily available in compact disc form, but to what extent can it be re-purposed? Few sound resources have been classified in terms of medium, content, original purpose, availability, NVQ-level and cost. On the other hand, the focus has to be on creating new sound samples rather than digitizing those from existing cassettes. The advantage of digital multimedia has to be the integration of sound with pictures, rather than sound itself. (For an existing digital audio laboratory model, see Appendix J.)

Video and satellite material
Substantial resources of video (incorporating satellite) material exists, mostly discretely deposited in the language centres of universities and colleges for the educational use of students. However, it will be some time before existing video material will be in common use by interactive language courseware designers for three reasons:

1. Confusion over copyright (especially where there is the possibility of re-sale, or public viewing);

2. The high cost of digitising moving colour pictures means that careful editing of the footage beforehand is essential (expensive in time and the cost of expert assistance). Digital editing costs are reducing rapidly, however, and this may not be a problem in the near future;

3. There are currently too few professional interactive language courseware designers around and teachers need training before becoming fully proficient.

The obvious sources for visual material are television companies, such as Anglia television, or the BBC. However, television companies seem uncertain about waiving their copyright restrictions over the use of material, even for experimental 'one-off' projects. No company has a clear policy on allowing developers to use their material for re-sale in a particular multimedia program, or for public viewing. Approaching companies for the use of their training videos seems a less complicated path, since they may see some commercial benefit from having their logo constantly displayed to students studying languages around the world. Ultimately, it is unlikely that much video material can be re-purposed to fit a language learning programme (especially at the lower levels) and shots may have to be filmed separately at higher cost.

The development platform for ELOQUENT

The work in ELOQUENT requires the highest performance at the lowest cost on a platform that exists today. Furthermore, the prognosis that digital technology will triumph over analogue technology due to its flexibility and potentially lower costmakes that route more attractive than laserdisk, even though quality of sound and screen resoluion may have to be compromised.

The requirement for an 'interactive language learning environment' also effectively excludes systems to which a student can read, but not write, such as CD-i and CD-ROM. Given this specification, the Acorn Archimedes A540 with read and write magneto-optical drive is the best option for at least the first phase of the project because of its cost–performance advantages in this field. The first stage of development work was carried out on the following specification:

A540 with 4 mb RAM
120 SCSI disc + SCSI card
800 kb floppy drive
Multisync monitor
Boxed 3.5 MO drive
RISCOS 3
Replay.

However, this leaves the question of compatibility and portability with regard to other platforms unresolved.

Compatibility and portability issues

Multimedia materials for language learning promise to be an excellent solution to the learning needs of many disparate student groups in either a networked or a self-access stand-alone environment. They can, however, be expensive to produce and assemble into coherent courses. This implies that the materials to be developed must be re-usable by as large a student population as possible. A logical consequence of this is that, where possible, prevailing industry standards must be adhered to in both hardware and software, so that the developed materials are not confined to a single delivery platform.

Because the development platform is an Acorn Archimedes, it is important to investigate the means by which the developed materials could be made compatible with more widespread industry standards, such as *Windows 3.1* running on IBM PC compatible machines. This work takes on an added significance if we assume that the developed materials could eventually be available remotely via a network, and that the current *de facto* European standard for industrial work and training is the PC. Any consideration of networking must take into account *de facto* inter-networking standards such as TCP/IP (Transmission control protocol/Internet protocol) and consider the more recent proposals of OSI (Open systems interconnection) so that future possibilities of passing data between networks is left open.

Two possible strategies could be used to achieve the desired compatibility:

1. ASCII text files can be transferred easily between systems. For graphical resources, public domain translators such as *!Translator* and *!Creator* could be used to convert still pictures between the Acorn Sprite format, and the more commonly used GIF and TIFF formats. Slightly improved results could be obtained by using the *!ChangeFSI* software which is copyrighted to Acorn Computers and distributed on all RISCOS 3.1 machines. Other graphics formats could be handled using the Postscript format which is common to Acorn, IBM, and Apple machines and *Artworks* (Archimedes), *Correl Draw* (IBM PC), *Adobe Illustrator* (Mac) and *Aldus Freehand* can exchange vector graphics via encapsulated postscript (EPS) files. The translation and compression of video material is a more complex issue which requires some detailed investigation before practical solutions can be proposed. But JPEG (Joint Photographic Experts' Group) and MPEG (Moving Pictures Experts' Group) standards are likely to be at least involved in intermediate compression. Audio material is generally simple to move between standards, although some adjustments may be required to handle the differences between 8, 16, and 32 bit systems.

2. Custom software for some of the specific functions that the project requires could be written, and generally available authoring tools could be used for the production of courseware. This would have the advantage of using software tailor-made and optimized for the task which would enhance performance. Once the data files are available and the structure of the courseware has been planned, the construction of applications using generally available editors and program generators is relatively quick and easy. Alternatively, a software shell could be written to assemble the various components of the application under a common interface. If this shell was written in C or C++, it should be possible to port the source code to any system with a C compiler including IBM PC, Apple and Sun. A feasibility study would seek to determine the most

effective and practicable of these possible solutions, and establish a balance between the various demands.

Pilot courseware model

Curriculum specification for the project

ELOQUENT will produce the interactive pilot materials for Italian, Greek, German and English which reflect the syllabus of the City and Guilds of London Institute's new vocational modern language examination syllabus, which has been developed specifically for workers who are mobile within the Single European employment market. This syllabus also forms a module within the Technological Baccalaureate (Beginner's Level Curriculum Section B7 'Communication Skills in One Other Language'; TechBac Examination Handbook, CGLI, London, 1991):

Listening

1. Understand spoken job instructions

2. Understand oral descriptions of graphical/pictorial material

3. Understand directions given with the aid of maps, plans and sketches

4. Understand workday communication with employer, customer or fellow-worker

5. Understand communication by telephone, radio or tannoy

Reading

1. Read and interpret written job instructions

2. Read and interpret labelled graphical/pictorial material

3. Read and interpret maps, plans and sketches

Speaking

1. Converse about job instructions

2. Discuss graphical/pictorial material

3. Give spoken directions with aid of plans, maps and sketches

4. Make work-day conversation with employer, customer or fellow-worker

5. Make telephone calls

Writing

1. Record job instructions

2. Write directions with the aid of maps, plans and sketches

3. Write work-day messages for employer, customer or fellow-worker

4. Write records of messages received by telephone or radio

5. Complete work-related forms or proforma documents.

If we take the first part of the syllabus concerned with 'job instructions' for each of the four skills (reading, writing, listening and speaking), it is possible to construct a pilot interactive course module composed of hypermedia cards, as shown in Figure 6.

Module design features

The student has to be able to move freely between situations using the mouse to click on specific features, such as pausing to check grammar or slowing down the speech. The student should be able to click on any on-screen text (including instructions) to hear the sound of the words and record his or her voice so as to compare it with the model. Exercises should be available across all the four skills for each scene and tutorial help for explanations of 'difficult' sections. The student has to be able to opt either to carry out the exercise or to listen to a tutor explaining the grammar points as and when it suits him or her. The language of the module needs to be at the same level (approximately NVQ level II, here) throughout the different scenes. In brief, seven specific features need to be built into the design:

1. On-line tutorial;

2. Guided learning routes;

3. Self-testing, certification and assessment;

4. Grammatical support;

5. Own voice recording;

6. Printing options;

7. On-line packages, such as word processor, database, electronic mail and so on.

As a minimum specification, the program has to incorporate facilities expected in linear technologies such as video recorder, cassette recorder and microphone as well as those offered by other learning media, such as grammar book, pronunciation guide and so on. The program has to be user-friendly. For example, it should offer:

- Subtitles, on or off, with translation into own language, on or off;

- Sound on or off, for text on screen as well as video sound;

- Close-up of mouth, for pronunciation drills;

- Exercises for each scene;

- Click on icon to move on, or to go to main menu;

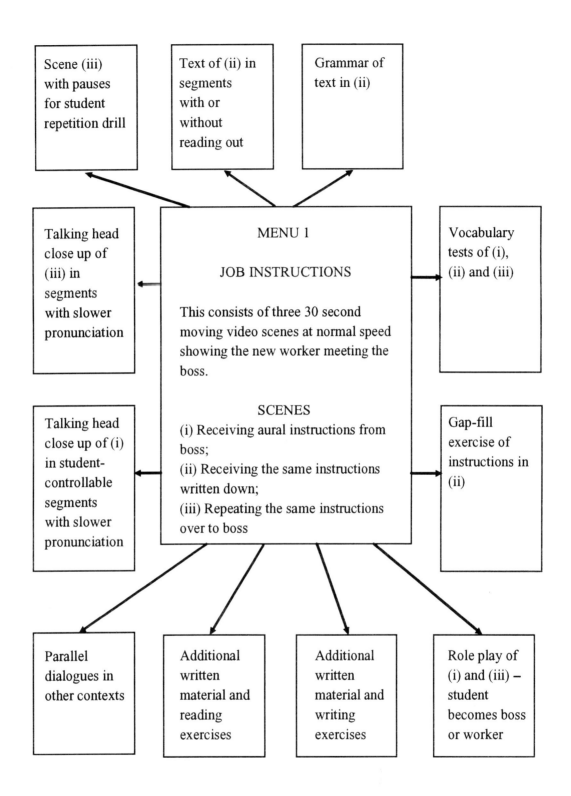

Figure 6. *Interactive course module: 'Learning job instructions'*

- Help box;

- Drill and practice routines such as role play, substitution exercises, gap-filling and word processing exercises;

- Grammar explanation;

- Slow sound box, for providing a slower received pronunciation model;

- Consistent screen layout and colouring.

Conclusions

Computer-based language learning is an emerging field where substantial work remains to be carried out.

High quality digitized moving pictures remain an essential goal to be reached within 18 months. Until then, digital video will always compare unfavourably with analogue, especially laserdisk-based programs. Technological difficulties of networking the material throughout Thomas Telford School and new methodologies of remote tutoring have yet to be trialled. Soon, however, when the confusion around copyright clears, agreements will be made that release a wealth of moving material which can be made into new language learning material cheaply through re-purposing techniques.

The implications for change in the language learning environment, identified in ELOQUENT, are profound. The whole approach to technology-based language learning will change with the emergence of new models of materials development, requiring a team of experts – linguist, programmer, human-computer interaction specialist, and teacher – and the development of new learning methodologies. Four tentative conclusions have been reached which provide general guidelines:

1. Multimedia is merely a delivery system: good multimedia design requires sensible methodological criteria from designers and language teachers to adapt their practical teaching and materials design experience to a new computer-based learning environment;

2. Choice of technology should be informed by the needs of the learner, i.e. the type of platform is irrelevant but the experience of the learner is foremost;

3. Technology is there to help learners, it should not be made to duplicate tasks which people, i.e. tutors, can do better;

4. New skills are needed to deliver technology-based language learning and training in new methodologies. For example, special resource staff would, with advice from tutors, compile the materials. This would then allow tutors to spend more time assessing progress and developing students' learning strategies.

Appendices

Appendix A: A short bibliography of current multimedia materials

The *ReCall Software Guide* published by the CTI Centre for Modern Languages, University of Hull, provides a comprehensive guide to other language-learning software, such as word processing, authoring tools, dictionaries, databases, and translation tools

Dedicated language-learning disks

Lingua-ROM: a *Hypercard* package including speech synthesis. Tutors basic concepts and constructs for Chinese, French, German, Italian, Russian, Spanish.

France Interactive developed by CALSA at Teesside University. Twenty learning modules, covering three levels of competence.

The European Connection: A series of discs produced by Vektor Ltd, and also marketed by Tandberg Educational: *The European Connection; La Connection Francaise; Die Deutsche Verbindung; La Conexion Espanola; The Personal Connection; The Meetings Connection.* Tandberg also markets voicecards and related tutoring programs and peripherals.

Paris En Video produced by the Educational Computing Consortium of Holland.

Siville: an Interactive Video disk produced by the UK Department of Trade and Industry to teach French.

Japanese for Business Travellers: a CD-i for tutoring Japanese to English-speaking businessmen, prepared by New Media/Vektor, funded by Department of Employment.

Japanese for Business Multimedia Corporation CD programme to tutor English to Japanese businessmen.

N.B. Further multimedia publications are expected during 1993 from MAST learning systems, Vektor Ltd. and Interactive Information Systems.

Dedicated language-learning software

Animez votre équipe. PC-based with VideoLogic overlay card, monitor and laserdisk player.

Ça y est. Homerton College CD-ROM, Cambridge.

French for Business. Apple Mac with CD-ROM drive.

Hotel Europa. Multimedia CD-ROMs for French, German and Spanish (PC-based).

Learn French with Asterix: Le Fils d'Asterix. Apple Mac (CD-ROM) and CDTV (Amiga) versions.

Expodisc Spanish. A PC-based interactive video system with VideoLogic card.

Available from Dida*El, via Lamarmora 3/A, I-20122 Milano, Italy:

Business Learning. This is a CBT course with four modules focussing on sales forecasts, pricing policies, the effects of pricing, and channels of distribution.

Basic English for the Office. This is a Hypercard program with a wide variety of exercises covering office English.

Italian for English-speaking people.

Authoring packages

Archimedes-based

Avanti (from Westland Systems, Yeovil). Designed for Acorn Archimedes series upwards Price £2150 for single developer's copy, not including educational discount.

GENESIS II (from Oak Solutions, Bradford). Designed for ease of use in school environment. Price £120.

Key Author (from Anglia TV). Integrates other Acorn products. Price £55.

Magpie (from Longman Logotron, Cambridge). Designed for schools at £39 per single user.

PC-based

GUIDE (3.1) (from Owl International, USA). Designed for 386 or 486, MS-DOS 4.0 version. Price $US695.

Multimedia Toolbook (1.5) (from Asymetrix Corporation, USA). Designed for use with 386, MS-DOS 3.1 or higher, *Windows 3.0* or higher. Can support *Hypercard* stacks. Price $US695.

Apple Mac

Hypercard (2.1) (from Claris International, Uxbridge). One of the first multimedia authoring packages. Price £35, also sold with Apple Mac machines.

Archival material and reference disks

Specific discs which may be useful resources for language learning include:

ECODISC. A CD-ROM with resources related to environmental studies with nine different languages available.

The BBC Doomesday IV disk.

Le Monde: *L'Histoire au Jour le Jour.* Archives of the newspaper, 1944-1985.

CEDROM Technologies disk *Textes et Contextes*, a database of extracts from French literary masterpieces.

Harraps *Multilingual Dictionary.* This contains eighteen separate dictionaries covering twelve languages.

Le Robert elecronique. This contains the 9000 pages of Le Grand Robert de la Langue Francaise.

Termdoc: a specialised technical dictionary offering equivalences for one hundred thousand terms in nine languages.

Appendix B: Technical specifications

Hardware specification of the language centres

Each of the centres has evolved its own combination of hardware resources to suit its approach and methodology:

George Stephenson Community High School

The hardware resources used at George Stephenson's School in Chapter I cover the breadth of technologies required for flexible learning; the specification combines older (but equally important) technologies, such as telephones (from BT) and cassette players, with more sophisticated technologies like interactive video. By following a lower-cost evolutionary path of adding new to old, the school still introduces students to all the media and fosters an understanding of how to use different technologies for different purposes:

Satellite television;

Video Camera – with playback and editing facilities;

4 telephones;

3 RM Nimbus computers + 2 printers;

1 Fast Copier, 1 Tape eraser;

2 OHPs;

Coomber recorders and headsets;

Micro cassette players and headsets;

2 TV / Video Recorders;

Electronic mail (access);

Interactive Video – access to digital and linear video technology;

ICL-sponsored resource centre and whole-school system.

The Brealey Languages Centre, St. George's School

The Brealey Languages Centre has chosen a high specification 27-workstation PC network as its core hardware on which it can build multimedia applications and carry out research and development, as well as offer teacher training to staff from LEAs and opted-out schools.

15 x Packard Bell IBM PC compatibles: ie
> 80386SX 16 MHz Processor
> 2 mb RAM
> 1 mb SVGA Monitor
> 40 mb Hard Drive
> 1 x 3.5" 1.44 mb floppy drive
> 8-bit Ethernet card
> + Voice Card

12 x Packard Bell IBM PC compatibles: As above, except
> 512k VGA display
> 1 x 5.25" 1.2 mb floppy disk

1 x Flatbed greyscale scanner

1 x CD-ROM drive

1 x Pace Quad (V32) modem.

NB The Centre still runs networks of 6 BBC 'B's, 15 x RM Nimbus 186s, 15 x BBC Master Compacts with Tandberg TCCR 530. The Central console control comprises 2 Tandberg TMU 502; 1 x SJ Research HDFS (20 mb) and 1 x SJ Research MDFS (40 mb) file servers and a Packard Bell 386 (120 mb).

Djanogly CTC Communications Centre

The Communications Centre at Djanogly CTC is notionally divided into two areas: language and computer; the 'language side' contains 24 laboratory places with AAC cassette decks and video monitors, controlled from the console. Video distribution enables students to receive satellite television pictures, video from the console, or images (e.g. text) captured by the video camera at the console. The other half of the Centre contains 24 audio cassettes, plus 24 networked Apricot 386 LAN (local area network) computers. The TECS system allows the teacher at the central console to control the PCs of students and talk to them via microphones.

Language Side of Centre: Hardware Spec

> 24 x positions IS10 Tandberg language laboratory (with video distribution + Microvitec monitor)
> + TECS computer interface
> Solara XLE satellite network

Teacher Console:

> Double Tutor with 2 master recorder models

Djanogly Recording Room

> 2 x small television isl 30
> 1 x fast copier
> 2 x VCRs
> 1 x Open Reel recorder
> Audio Mixer
> 2 video cameras.

Thomas Telford School: Acorn Digital Language Centre

The Thomas Telford multimedia language centre network has been designed to interface with the existing PC network so that students can download IBM-compatible programs from the main college network, as well as run interactive language learning applications on *GENESIS II*. This is the first stage of a digital language laboratory, where tapes have become obsolete and pictures and sound are digitised (see Chapter IV):

> Network: 12 x Acorn A5000's (with 80 mb HDs)
> GENESIS II from Oak Solutions Ltd.
> 12 Oak Recorders with Microphones
> 4mb RAM
> 16-bit Ethernet card
> 486 Novell Netware Fileserver running TCPIP
> (from PC network)

The Archimedes A540 platforms for courseware development running *GENESIS II* are specified in Chapter IV, but the intention is that students and staff will eventually be able to use the network to develop their own materials at a later stage, when magneto-optical drives will be installed.

Language centre layouts and furnishing

Each of the centres has either customized, or specialist rooms, with purpose-built storage facilities. The rationale for this is simply that the nature of language learning requires facilities which can cope with

1. Adequate electrical provision;

2. Secure, lockable storage cupboards to protect the valuable learning resources and movable equipment from damage and theft;

3. Sound proofing eg (acoustic tiles and anti-static flooring) to accommodate the higher level of decibels generated from frequent and loud dialogue and oral practice.

4. The language centre should itself be located away from noisy areas of the school because of the frequent need for intensive listening practice.

There is, however, another important spin-off; the existence of a location specifically designated for language learning gives greater status to the subject itself within the school; it demonstrates in a tangible way the value the school places on language learning. It may be the case that in future language learning will take place at the multimedia workstation anywhere on the premises at any time, rather than in a specially-designated area. Where this has been introduced, it has received a mixed reception; students studying other less vocal subjects nearby feel disrupted and those at the language workstations tend to feel inhibited by the presence of onlookers and practise their oral language less frequently.

Layouts can vary significantly. At one time there was just the languages classroom; then a language laboratory with booths in serried rows was installed and now the an open plan system, where students can move freely from one activity to another, is increasingly popular. Benches tend either to be placed around the periphery of the room to allow for activity in the centre, or shaped into hexagonal mushrooms, which encourages interaction such as group and pair-work. The Brealey Languages Centre, for example, is open plan with the control console in the centre of the room and 17 tables clustered in 'mushrooms' around the console, while the Djanogly Communications Centre occupies an open-plan space equivalent to three classrooms, notionally divided into three zones; audio/video stations on mushroom tables in one zone; the interpreting suite around the wall of another; and the computer/CD-ROM workstations on parallel benches in the third. Further designs of language classrooms and centres appear in Appendix H.

Appendix C: Approximate costings

The main PC network at the Brealey Languages Centre

Hardware	Approximate cost
2 x IBM PC compatibles: 80386DX 33MHz Processor 8 mb RAM 200 mb Hard Drive Mono VGA Display 16-bit Ethernet card (fileservers)	£1200 each
15 x IBM PC compatibles: 80386SX 16MHz Processor 4 mb RAM 1 mb SVGA Display 40 mb Hard Drive 1 x 3.5" 1.44 mb Floppy Drive 8-bit Ethernet card	
12 x IBM PC compatibles: As above specification except 512k VGA display 4 mb RAM 1 x 5.25" 1.2 mb Floppy Drive	£800–£900 each
1 x Tandberg Voice Card	£170
1 x Flatbed GrayScale scanner	£1000
1 x CD-ROM Drive	£500
1 x Advanced gravis ultrasound card	£140
1 x Pace Quad (V32) modem	£500

Software	Approximate cost
Novell Netware 2.15 (100 user)	£2000
Novell Netware 3.11 (20 user)	£1300
Works for DOS	£80
Works for Windows	£80
Linkway v2.0	
Tick-Tack	
Thinksheet	
Pegasus mail (e-mail)	Freeware
Chat (2-person conferencing)	Shareware

CD-ROMs	Approximate cost
Hotel Europa France	£60
Harraps multilingual dictionary database	£600
Zyzomys	£415
Alde Spectrum Clipart	£200

Djanogly CTC communications centre

Costs for the first stage of the installation in 1989

N.B.

- The PC network and the interpreting suite are not included;

- Costs are approximate;

- All prices were calculated in collaboration with Tandberg in the initial stage of planning. The final installation had some modifications and additions.

Within the languages area (24 positions) cost per pupil:

Example A

IS10 + Electronics	£660.00
Video Distribution System	£90.00
Extra Headsets	£35.00
Computer Interface (optional)	£100.00
Microvitec Monitor (graphics and video)	£525.00
Total per pupil	£1,416.00
Giving a total for 24 positions of	£33,984.00

Example B

As above, but with a monitor giving only video and television pictures

	£235.00
Revised total per pupil	£1,126.00
Giving a total for 24 positions of	£27,024.00

N.B. If, at a later date, it was decided to install computers, the cheaper monitor would have to be replaced.

Example C

For greater student control and playback video facility with teacher control, each station should also have a VCR. Without this the video system is relatively limited

VCR (each)	£230.00
24 VCRs	£5,520.00
Total cost	£39,584.00
with Microvetic for television and video only	£32,547.00

Example D

12 VCRs only	£2,760.00
Total with Microvitec	£36,744.00
Television/video only	£29,784.00

Example E

£2,400 could be deducted from these figures if computer interface electronics was omitted

IT area (cost per pupil)

IS10 Electronics	£666.00
Computer Interface	£100.00
Total per pupil	£766.00
Total for 24 positions	£18,394.00

N.B. The remaining hardware to be calculated as part of the IT budget:

Running total (maximum)	£39,584.00
+	£18,094.00
Total (maximum)	£57,978.00
Running total (minimum)	£29,784.00
+	£18,394.00
-	£2,400.00
Total (minimum)	£45,778.00

Satellite network

Solara XLE – three dishes European/Soviet Intelsat/Eutelsat plus cabling, receiving and fitting (approximately)	£2,000.00
Total (maximum)	£59,978.00
Total (minimum)	£47,778.00

Recording Room

2 x small television isl 30 @ £239.00 each	£478.00
1 x fast copier – Gem Crystal	£1,395.00
2 x VCRs @ £250.00 each	£500.00
1 x open reel recorder	£575.00
1 x audio mixer	£400.00
Total	£3,348.00

Running total (maximum)	£63,326.00
Running total (minimum)	£51,126.00

Extras

2 x video cameras @ £1,400 each	£2,800.00
1 x VCR in master console	£250.00
Total	£3,050.00

Running total (maximum)	£66,376.00
Running total (minimum)	£54,176.00

Teacher master console (double tutor with two master recorder models)
estimated cost   £10,000.00
Sound proofing and double glazing in recording room estimated cost
                                                               £7,000.00
Furniture   £12,000.00

Total (maximum)   £95,376.00
Total (minimum)   £83,176.00

Appendix D: Links between programmes of study in IT capability and in modern foreign languages

IT capability (technology AT5) PoS statements	Related MFL PoS statements
Pupils should be taught:	**Pupils should have regular opportunities to:**
• that information technology can be used to help plan and organize ideas in written and graphical form (KS1)	• record and express information in different forms... for different audiences (KS3 and KS4)
	• produce a variety of types of writing (KS3 and KS4)
• how to store, select and analyse information using software, for example, using a simple database (KS1)	• conduct surveys and other investigations in the class, school or outside (KS3 and KS4)
• to organize, develop amd present ideas in a variety of forms by using software packages (KS2)	• redraft and existing written text (including their own) for a different audience or purpose (KS3 and KS4)
• to put existing information into a new format (KS2)	
• to work together to prepare and present stored information using information technology (KS2)	• plan and carry out practical and creative activities with a partner or in a group (KS3 and KS4)
• to use information technology for investigations requiring the analysis of data (KS2)	• investigate, discuss and report on aspects of the language and culture of these countries or communities (KS4)
• to use information technology to work more effectively (KS3)	• redraft their own writing to improve its accuracy and presentation (KS3 and KS4)
• to select software for a task or application (KS3)	• develop independence in their choice of tasks, materials and use of equipment (KS3 and KS4)
• to know that the use of information technology does not always provide an appropriate solution to a need, and that the effectiveness, appropriateness and cost of alternative solutions must be considered (KS3)	• use a range of reference materials and resources (KS3 and KS4)
• to review and discuss their use of information technology and consider applications in the outside world, and the impact on daily life, including environment, ethical, moral and social issues (KS4)	• explore AoE E (KS3 and KS4)

Source: National Curriculum Council (1992)

Appendix E:
Satellite televisions and communications – their place in the modern languages classroom

Janet Jones, Brooke College, Corby

Satellite television has been around for long enough now for some to feel blasé about it and for others to feel that they can still afford to ignore it because it has no prescribed role under National Curriculum targets.

Is it really just a gimmick or can it be seen as a resource to be harnessed to support innovative teaching in a situation where preparation of material means that time is at a premium?

A closer look at the National Curriculum documents reminds us that the context of the world of communications and the international world are target areas of study. These have often been ignored in the past because of their inaccessibility. In an era when many students are familiar with satellite technology it would be foolish to pretend such a resource did not exist.

Is it a practical resource for the teacher in the classroom? I believe it to be the most effective way to date of bringing the chosen language and culture into the classroom. The knowledge absorbed by students is far in excess of the narrow bands of linguistic competence.

The skill in developing the resource does, in the first instance, require some investment of time. To be familiar with the technology is a relatively easy step if the system installed has been carefully planned and no 'mystique' has been allowed to develop. It is after all just the big brother version of what most of us use at home.

Getting to know the programming, both commercial and educational takes a bit longer. Here too, however, we often underestimate what students enjoy and what they are capable of. There is no requirement for the language to be at the level of learner; it is more important that the visual material supports the language and that the pace of language allows the successful completion of the chosen task.

The reviewing of material is often seen as the major headache for many members of staff but here again, a little bit of investment in terms of time should mean that a bank of materials can be built up and used in a variety of ways. News broadcasts can be recorded on a regular basis to form a library of topical material which can be kept up to date and which gives more experienced learners the opportunity to handle topical and often new vocabulary in context. The value of this should not be underestimated for teaching staff either who wish to keep their language fluency.

Any items of value can then be edited out for a topic resource base as required. In addition to this, it is relatively easy to identify likely material for student use. A video clip should be chosen for its clarity, brevity, visual support and entertainment level. The motivation factor here is a strong card to play in keeping students stimulated to take their language learning further.

The teacher does not necessarily need to see every piece of television. Once the format of the programme is known to be suitable it is possible to ask students to review recordings at whatever level is appropriate. Some staff use a prepared grid for this purpose, others might use a series of open-ended questions to elicit information.

In considering satellite television the text available at the same time should not be forgotten. If this can be accessed too, and there are a number of ways of doing this, another information resource is accessible by staff and students alike. As suggested above, students can be asked to check on weather reports, top ten charts, recipes, news bulletins and the like depending on the area of study.

Not all commercial material is suitable for use in school, but a great deal has more to offer than may at first be realised. In addition there are the specialist education channels on a variety of satellites. Educational programming is regarded by students in a different way and therefore needs to be handled in a different way. Here the opportunities are those of broadcast packages in line with National Curriculum topics, the opportunity to interact with other learners via satellite television pictures and a computer whiteboard or by audio-conferencing.

Not only students benefit from this kind of technology. Staff too can come together relatively easily to discuss and develop ideas in an INSET situation. The visual support offered by broadcast communications has a strong impact on the participant but does not involve staff or schools in long journeys and high training costs.

A school or college thinking of investing or developing this resource in the near future needs to spend some time planning the requirements of the institution because satellite communications ought to be seen as a whole school resource and because the most vital element in ensuring its successful integration is its availability to staff and students alike.

Choosing equipment is always going to depend on the individual needs of the establishment but there are some guidelines which might prove useful.

- If more than one curriculum area is likely to use the facility, the receiver will need to be linked to a series of videos which can record the required material. A single receiver dish will only be able to record from one satellite at a time.

- Several languages are available on several different channels but some channels carry a much better service than others; it is therefore important, for example, not to be persuaded by sales talk that 'French' is only available on one satellite. To access the best material and facilites available at the moment, you will need to be able to tune to Eutelstat, Telecom and Olympus.

- The size of dish required will depend on the geographical location of the institution and the local conditions and it will need a clear southerly aspect. It is also important to consider the siting of the dish from a maintenance point of view.

- The most effective system will therefore be sited at a vandal-proof position with a clear aspect across the immediate buildings and will be able to track the range of satellites broadcasting their footprint within range of the dish and the receiver will be able to handle the different broadcast formats: PAL and D2-MAC.

In return for the investment of time and money the school has at its disposal a resource which remains stimulating, up to date and interactive. The reward is in the broad range of experience which can be offered to both student and staff.

Appendix F:
Attitude survey of technology-based flexible learning at George Stephenson Community High School

Student views

George Stephenson Community High School students were asked to comment on what they thought of flexible learning. When asked whether they liked or disliked the wayof working, the majority had very positive views. The relative number of quotations being 'for' and 'against' reflects the general balance of opinion. A few negative opinions were expressed, which were mainly concernded with the lack of computer availability and teacher time.

For:

- 'You have your own time to listen to tapes etc.' 'Everything combines together to help you, e.g. listening improves speaking' (female, set 4);
- 'I enjoyed the interactive video because it was different and interesting. I liked the moving pictures combined with sound' (male, set 3);
- 'You don't have to stick at the same ting all of the time' (female, set 2);
- 'Makes learning more interesting and enjoyable' (male, set 3);
- 'The listening is good because we learn how to pronounce words' (female, set 1);
- 'The satellite and video help you learn more about life in France and Germany, and the countries themselves' 'The computer makes learning fun but you still learn' 'Reading, listening etc are authentic' (female, set 1);
- 'Work at your own speed' 'The telephones make conversation more fun and more realistic' (male, set 2);
- 'It's good for you as you have responsibility' (male, set 1);
- 'There's a lot of work to get on with and a wide range of activities to do' 'The tapes are good because you can rewind and fast forward it' (male, set 2);
- 'You get a choice of what you can do' (female, set 2);
- 'The computer helps vocabulary a lot' (male, set 3)
- 'The computer is good for fact learning' (male, set 3);
- 'Fun to do' (female, set 1);
- 'Working on your own helps you understand' (male, set 2);
- 'The computer helps your vocabulary learning, verbs and tenses' (female, set 3);
- 'You don't feel pressure from the teacher' 'You learn from the computer – it makes writing much more interesting' (male, set 2, normally quite disruptive!);
- 'I like the way the teacher doesn't walk around the classroom like a prison warden and stop people form talking' (male, set 3);
- 'Doesn't embarass you when you do something wrong' (male, set 3);
- 'You don't have to keep up with someone faster or hold back for slower people' (male, set 1);

- 'Variety' 'Chance to work with others' 'Good class co-operation' 'If you are shy, practising oral work in two's makes it less embarrassing' (female, set 1);
- 'Working independently is good because you can get on with work' 'Oral work is quite good fun' (female, set 2);
- 'When you are in a group doing oral work you learn more' (male, set 4).

Against:

- 'It would get very boring if we did this every lesson' (female, set 1);
- 'Too many in class' 'Teacher always seems busy' (female, set 1);
- 'There should be more computers' (male, set 2);
- 'Sometimes you get distracted and talk' 'People might bag equipment' 'You could do more of one thing than the other' (male, set 3);
- 'Don't get to use the computers as often as I would like because other people are on them' (female, set 2).

Staff perceptions

Advantages:

- 'The personalized relationship between teacher and student';
- 'The personalized help given openly to each individual which disguises differences between students in intellect or ability. Consequently, students do not feel inadequate';
- 'Students learning to be organized and methodical as well as being responsible for their own learning. It also develops an independent and enquiring mind';
- 'Maximizes student output';
- 'Relaxed working atmosphere';
- 'Students are responsible for setting up and managing their own learning';
- 'It allows differentiation';
- 'It allows a mixing of skills and media';
- 'It frees more teacher time for profiling, counselling and one-to-one oral work';
- 'It reduces the problem of teacher absence';
- 'Individual has the scope to work at his or her own areas of weakness. The teacher can respond to need';
- 'Owing to an improvement in personal responsibility there is an overall improvement in discipline';
- 'When there is a teacher absence, substituting teachers have only to unlock the door. The youngsters do the rest';
- 'There is a good atmosphere in the classroom and it is active and busy. Students see the teacher as a facilitator and a tutor. There is enthusiasm for working in this way'.

Disadvantages:

- 'The teacher needs to ensure that no time is wasted when settling down or when changing activities... the non-work related chats are reduced to a minimum...';
- 'The teacher needs to ensure that a methodical approach is being acquired; noting unknown vocabulary, listening in the way that has been advised, effective use of dictionary';
- 'Difficult to supervise individual work or test individually because at that time no help can be given to the rest of the group...';
- 'Some students look for an easy life';
- 'It demands more of teachers' organizational skills';
- 'The teacher needs to be constantly and consistently insistent about detail';
- 'Setting up this way of working is initially time-consuming. The students also have to be drilled so that they respect the organization and work within it';
- 'Equipment has to be used responsibly and it all has to be put back in exactly the right place';
- 'The first two or three lessons are the most difficult. After that, the students begin to understand what they are doing and they make it work';
- 'Although the students themselves are responsible for doing most of this, careful monitoring is needed to ensure that it is taking place. The teacher also needs to be sure that enough time is being allocated in appropriate skill areas. Doing this on an individual basis is initially quite difficult but once they begin to identify what they need, it works well';
- 'Machinery can break down but this has not been a serious problem'.

Appendix G:
A checklist for modern language teaching facilities

The modern languages suite

- Specialist rooms, 'en suite'

- Small teaching spaces included

- Purpose-built storage facilities

- Secure storage for expensive equipment

- Adequate ventilation, temperature 15-20°C in storage areas

- Library storage for audio visual cassettes

- Wall-mounted wallchart storage

- Department office/recording room, with:
  - Minimum of 4 double power points

  - Word processing facility

  - Computer terminal

  - Telephone line and modem

  - Recording equipment

  - TV and VHF/FM aerials and radio-cassette recorder, with timer, for recording 'off-air', if no central recording arrangements available

  - Minimum of two 4-drawer filing cabinets

The modern languages classroom

- Optimum size = $4m^2$ per 2 pupils

- Almost square or L-shaped

- One window wall, down one of longer sides

- Good acoustic properties:
  - sited away from noisy areas

  - anti-static carpeting

  - acoustic tiles on ceiling/walls

- Minimum of 8 double power points:
  - situated around perimeter of room

  - two or three double points at front

  - two or three double points on remaining walls, at desk top height

- Adequate lighting

- Dimmer switch at front of room

- Dim-out provided, curtains or roller blinds

- Adequate display areas, display boards

- Whiteboard (dry marker pens) fitted

- Fixed overhead projection screen

- Floor mounted cupboards with pull-out trays

- Benching/work-surface around perimeter

Furniture

- Durable, lightweight stackable chairs and tables

- Large, lockable teacher's desk

- 1 audio-visual trolley per room

- Area with easy chairs

Equipment

- 1 good quality cassette recorder/player per room

- 2 wall-mounted extension speakers, or 1 high specification amplifying loudspeaker

- Minimum of 2 small cassette recorders with group listening facilities

- Overhead projector

- Overhead projector trolley

Available within department:

- Bulk/fast cassette copier

- TV monitor on purpose-built trolley

- Video-recorder or video play-back machine with remote control

- Computer workstation on purpose-built trolley

- Internal telephone link

- Slide/filmstrip projector

and access to good reprographic facilities

Source: National Association of Language Advisers, *Equiping the Modern Languages Department*, 1989:19-20

Appendix H: Example room layouts

This appendix contains six diagrams which suggest alternative room layouts for language centres. These diagrams are presented in Figures H1 to H6:

Figure H1. The modern languages suite;

Figure H2. The modern languages resources area in Dereham Neatherd High School, Norfolk;

Figure H3. The 'Herringbone' language classroom design;

Figure H4. The 'Double Horseshoe' language classroom design;

Figure H5. Two layouts for self-access centres;

Figure H6. Suggested layouts for listening and language centre facilities.

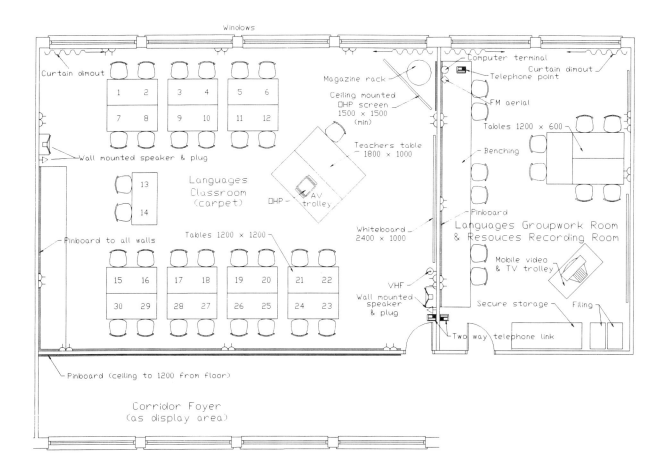

Figure H1. *The modern languages suite (NALA, 1989:18)*

Design of centre: The room is equipped with eight listening booths, each with its own tape recorder and headphones. In this area there are also tables to seat about 12 pupils. The teacher's desk has an overhead projector and a screen behind. Storage space with shelves displaying books and magazines and drawers with tapes acts as a partial room divider, separating the listening and writing area from the other more informal part of the room. This area is furnished with a settee, armchairs and bean bags and is an area where pupils can talk in groups or in pairs, work with the teacher or language assistant on oral work or watch a video. On the opposite wall to the listening booths is a long shelf where the computers stand. The telephones are another important resource which can be plugged in and used for extra practice in authentic oral situations and which can be used in conjunction with a tape recorder.

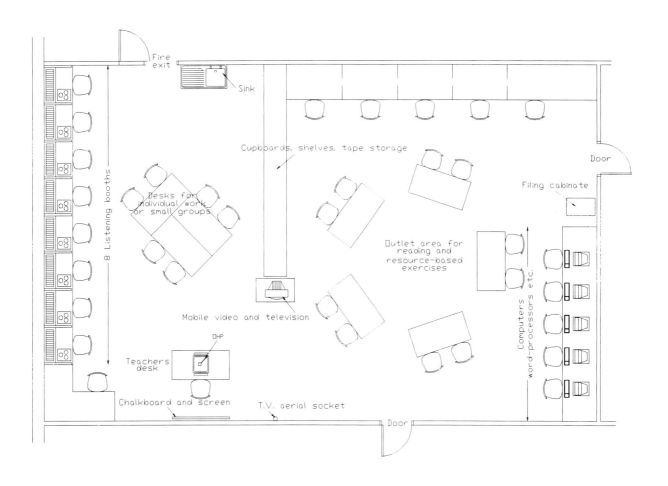

Figure H2. *The modern languages resources area in Dereham Neatherd High School, Norfolk (Goddard and Harding, 1991:10)*

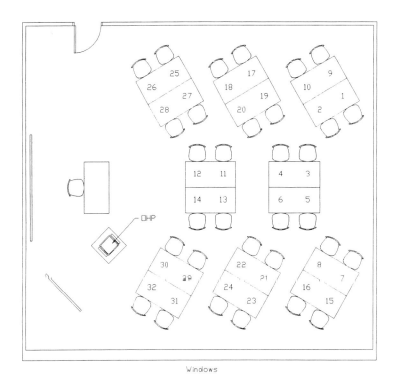

Figure H3. *The 'Herringbone' language classroom design*
(NALA, 1989, p. 7)

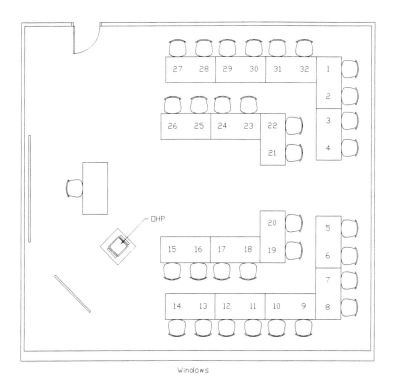

Figure H4. *The 'Double Horseshoe' language classroom design*
(NALA, 1989, p. 8)

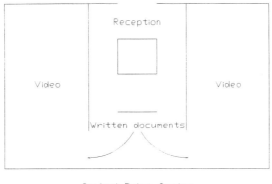

Central Entry System

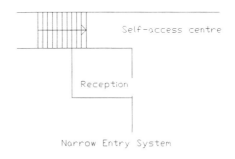

Narrow Entry System

Figure H5. *Two layouts for self-access centres*

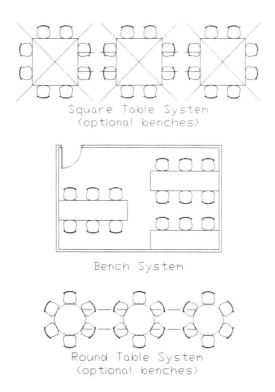

Figure H6. *Suggested layouts for listening and language centre facilities (based on Little (1989: 50/51)*

Appendix I: Specification for the latest type of audio-active comparative language laboratory

Console

- Advanced touch screen or push button control of all functions;
- Capable of handling up to 80 students (including remote stations);
- Four teaching groups with additional library mode;
- Full random or automatic pairing facility;
- Model voice or multiple voice facility;
- Five video inputs as standard on the language laboratory with facility to output to two large classroom monitors and teacher monitors;
- Computerized student attendance facility;
- Four times normal transmission of programme with programme pause facility;
- Programme mute facility while transmitting programme;
- Student microphone mute facility while transmitting programme;
- Teacher monitor speaker;
- Dual headset facility on teaching console;
- Dual position master recorders with book mark (five book marks);
- Teacher book mark can be transmitted to student position;
- Lid lock facility to classroom;
- Console has two power settings: one for self-access or library mode, the other for full classroom teaching;
- The system also corresponds to stereo or bi-lingual programme sources;
- Interpretation exercises can be conducted on the system;
- Full self-diagnostics of the system are fitted as standard;
- Remote control operation of the teacher console can be achieved with additional board;
- Optional fully-programmable editor;
- Optional student analyser
- Optional video distribution to individual students.

Student recorder

- Single touch button student operation;
- Fast cue and review option plus single touch for pause;
- Full random five point index mark;
- A and B repeat facility;
- Sentence repeat facility;
- LCD master display;
- Tape speed control +/- 12%;
- Left and right balance facility when in stereo mode;
- Call facility;
- Teacher student balance adjustment;
- Volume control;
- Programme select button when system has video distribution.

Appendix J:
A voice card language laboratory model

Background

In 1991, the University College of North Wales, Bangor designed and installed a voice card language laboratory as a replacement for its old cassette-based model (Wright, 1992). This appendix describes the problems encountered during installation and the chosen solution for each.

Specification

Hardware:

- 20 student positions with Elonex 386SM (slimline);
- Tandberg Tecs system – Teleste 1000 cards (sampling rate = 20,000 Hz);
- 40mb hard disk;
- Sun fileservers (on the college network).

Software:

- PC-NFS specially adapted version copying to workstations at 6mb per minute;
- PKZIP file compression;
- 'Oyez!' teaching software.

Teething troubles and solutions

Problem: Installing the computer into existing compact language laboratory furniture.

Solution: Slimline computers mounted vertically on shelves below desks.
Monitors remounted on tubular bases 11cm in diameter.

Problem: Noise!

Solution: Acoustic tiles, heavy curtains and thick carpets were fitted;
Computers partially boxed and tucked away under student desks;
Master recordings are made on a separate computer to avoid sound interference from the surrounding workstations;
Use of headsets can reduce monitor and fan buzz.

Problem: Memory of file transfer and storage

Solution: The files only occupy 600mb on the fileserver so when required an extra drive is added and unused files transferred to a tape streamer;
Audio files are copied to hard disks of workstations beforehand.
A hard disk (not the fileserver) is used for the teaching software;
Caching on the fileserver enables 10 workstations to be copied to in the same time as it would take to copy to one.

Problem: Staff preparation time

Solution: Class material initially takes a long time, but quality is never lost and digital recordings are easily stored and manipulated to fit new exercises.

Appendix K:
Review of multimedia platforms and authoring systems for language learning

The following is an extract from *Designing Interactive Multimedia to Support Language Learning*, a report commissioned for ELOQUENT, published January 1993, pp 16–20.

The multimedia market now offers a wide choice of delivery platforms, storage media, peripheral devices and authoring programs. With the growth of the consumer market, there is now also an intriguing choice of relatively low-cost delivery systems designed for the home, which may also be profitably used in education.

Laserdisk systems

Interactive video (IV) systems normally combine video and audio and come from a 30cm/12" Laserdisk, and the complementary control program, text and graphics from a computer disk. A typical hardware configuration includes a Laserdisk player, a computer, a monitor, and an input device such as keyboard or mouse, with optional accessories such as headphones or speakers.

The computer usually employs an plug-in overlay card to mix the otherwise incompatible audio-visual signals from the Laserdisk player with the digital data from the computer for output to the screen and speakers. Most interactive video packages are based on PCs but, within education, packages have been developed for use with Acorn, Macintosh and PC-compatible computers.

Laserdisk systems still represent the best medium for high-quality moving pictures, which still challenge the storage and processing capacities of compact discs and hard disks, so IV is a good system where the visual content requires a lot of video. Laserdisks are, however, tied to national broadcasting standards.

Examples of interactive video in language learning include the Vektor Connections series (for example, *La Connection Française*).

Multimedia systems

The new generation of multimedia system usually integrate audio, visual and computer resources on a single medium for processing within a single box. There are now computers with integral CD-ROM drives, and boxes dedicated to specific CD formats such as CD-i and CDTV.

Compact disk (CD) technology is based on the principle of upward compatibility, so all CD-based platforms have some features in common. This means that, for example, all CD systems are constrained by retrieval and processing speeds which are relatively slow by comparison to contemporary computer systems, but that many CD formats are essentially compatible. All the other CD drives so far developed will play the familiar CD digital audio discs (CD-DA), and many will also accept the new Photo CD format.

The Multimedia PC (MPC)

The Multimedia PC (MPC) standard was established during 1992 by a consortium of hardware and software companies led by Microsoft. It is by no means an official standard, but represents a reasonable specification for multimedia on the desktop computer, and supports a range of trademarked delivery systems, upgrade kits and compatible software (including education titles). The MPC standard calls for a PC with: 386SX processor, at least 2MB of RAM, 80MB hard disk drive, BGA monitor, sound card, CD-ROM card and, if interactive video is also being used, an overlay card as well.

Phillips, for instance, offer an MPC system with a 120MB hard disk, the Media Vision audio board, and their latest CM 205 CD-ROM drive, which has XA capability. The machine has a modular architecture which can be upgraded to be a 486 machine.

More generally, the MPC specification offers a good model for the upgrade of other computer systems, or the design of a multimedia delivery system based on other computer platforms.

CD-Digital Audio (CD-DA)

The most familiar CD format offers a choice of high-quality or large capacity for audio storage. Published music discs employ the high level of quality, which offers some 72 minutes or so of audio per disc, but other techniques provide many hours of recordings of lower quality. The discs can be played in other CD drives, and can thus be linked to computers to support language learning packages such as *French for Business* on the Apple Macintosh.

Compact Disc Interactive (CD-i)

CD-i was released by Philips as a consumer product in Europe during April 1992, some six months after its debut in the US. It is a single-box system which connects to the television. At present, it supports text, stills, animation, audio and computer data; moving video should be introduced during 1993 (although the introduction of this feature has already been postponed more than once), and the current generation of players could then be upgraded to include video.

CD-i players tend to be controlled by infra-red devices such as the joystick, mouse or graphic tablet, although other devices are being developed which will fit into the communication ports on the back of the player.

CD-i employs its own technical standard, based on CD but refined through features including a unique real-time operating system, CD-RTOS. This means that any CD-i disc can be played on any CD-i player anywhere in the world. However, users accustomed to the rapid responses of dedicated computer games, for example, may find CD-i – and, indeed, other systems based on compact disc technology – slow by comparison in applications where rapid interaction is expected.

A single CD-i disc supports up to 16 separate audio tracks at one time, so CD-i could offer many languages, dialects or accents on one disc. The only CD-i language disc created in the UK so far was designed as a research disc with funding from the UK's Department of Employment, and so is not available commercially.

Commodore Dynamic Total Vision (CDTV)

CDTV – now officially rebraded as Amiga CDTV – is based on Commodore's Amiga computer. It was launched as a consumer product in the UK in 1991 and, after a slow year in the home entertainment market, repositioned within the Amiga home computer range in 1992. It is a single-box system which can play CD- DA and CDTV discs, displaying these images on an ordinary television.

Amiga CDTV supports audio, stills, text, graphics, animation, and computer data, and should introduce moving video facilities during 1993. Like other CD-based systems, Amiga CDTV has slower response times than a fast desktop computer, but, appears to integrate audio-visual facilities more effectively than many computers.

The CDTV catalogue favours games, children's titles and reference materials. The only titles in the area of language learning are the *Asterix* series, which are also available for use on the Macintosh computer.

Compact Disc–Read Only Memory (CD-ROM)

Where CD-DA typically offers relatively low storage capacity in return for extremely high data quality, CD-ROM reverses the equation to offer large-volume storage for text, simple graphics and audio recordings, numeric and other data. CD-ROM is designed to hold large quantities of information at relatively low levels of audio- visual quality, and to deliver this information quickly through large and often complex retrieval facilities. Thus, CD-ROM is typically used to store databases, reference materials and other large textual collections.

CD-ROM's limited facility for audio-visual material is answered by CD-ROM XA (below) and the various multimedia CD formats. As a medium for use in language learning, CD-ROM is particularly useful for the storage of dictionaries and other reference material, of which there are many examples commercially available.

Compact Disc–ROM eXtended Architecture (CD-ROM XA)

CD-ROM has limitations for the delivery of fully integrated multimedia presentations, which the extended architecture of the XA platform addresses. CD-ROM XA employs standards for encoding graphics, audio and still pictures, developed from CD-i. Thus, while CD-ROM stores and processes text, graphics and still pictures in separate blocks, CD-ROM XA interleaves data of different types to produce presentations which are faster and smoother than conventional CD-ROM.

XA supports both CD-i's CD-Real Time Operating System (CD-RTOS) and the industry-standard Microsoft Disk Operating System (MS-DOS). Therefore, an XA disc could be used in the PC at work, and the CD-i player at home – at least, in theory, for there is still little evidence of the 'bridge libraries' of development software and published titles to bridge the gap between the two systems.

However, XA was recognised as a platform in its own right with the launch in the US in the autumn of 1992 of Sony's new portable multimedia player, MMCD. This system uses the XA standard to publish a variety of multimedia titles for business, reference and education on compact disc; it has already won the support of several important electronic publishers, with a choice of some 60 titles for Christmas 1992.

Tandy Video Information System (VIS)

This single-box multimedia player – which, like CD-i and Amiga CDTV, plugs into a television or stereo system – was launched in the US in 1992, and is scheduled to reach Europe during 1993. It is now a home entertainment produce like CD-i and Amiga CDTV, but its architecture is designed to accommodate interactive communication through telephone lines, cable, satellite and other devices which Tandy believe will be integrated into homes, schools and the workplace within the next decade. This, too, is a watching brief with no immediate relevance for language learning, but tremendous potential for distance learning and communications in the future.

Desktop Video (DTV)

Today's multimedia learning packages expect to use still and moving video and sound – all of which take up enormous quantities of storage space when every second of PAL video running at full speed demands 25 separate frames. Each frame is effectively a still picture which, as a computer graphic, requires at least 290KB of memory in storage terms, and also requires memory for the process of getting the material to the screen in a seamless presentation. This was until recently, therefore, a strong case for linking up a Laserdisk player to the computer and calling up analogue video from the Laserdisk player whenever photographic images were required.

However, compression techniques to reduce the volume of data required to store and process photographic images are developing rapidly. Formal standards are emerging for still and moving pictures from the Jint Photographic Experts Group (JPEG) and the Motion Pictures Experts Group (MPEG) of the International Standards Organisation (ISO). Several hardware manufacturers and software developers have also developed compression systems – some based on the work of JPEG and MPEG, others employing unique standards and techniques. Some of these products employ hardware (particularly, add-on boards for the computer) while others are effected through software alone. Many address the challenge of full-screen, full-motion video (FMV) by containing the display within a window on the screen (i.e. less than full- screen) or at a slower speed than broadcast-standard video (i.e. less than full-motion), and often at a lower quality than television or even VHS video.

Thus, there is typically a trade-off between the quantity and quality of the video, and the cost and facility with which it is produced, which each development team must evaluate within the context of their own project. With all video, the quality of the final display reflects the quality of the source material, the way in which it was processed, and capabilities of the hardware which ultimately delivers it (particularly, the quality of the monitor itself).

Digital Video Interactive (DVI) Technology

DVI technology was developed by a series of manufacturers before other desktop DVI technology was developed by a series of manufacturers before other desktop video facilities or multimedia platforms were available. It is therefore based on its own unique standards and algorithms, and is now incorporating other standards which have more recently emerged the computer and multimedia industries at large (notably, JPEG and MPEG).

DVI technology is a process rather than a product – a set of chips which allow video and still pictures to be compressed and decompressed entirely within the computer. As compressed video resources demand large-volume storage, this material is often on a CD rather than on the computer's harddisk. Developers can create and process all this material themselves – typically, shooting still and moving pictures on film or video and then digitising the images for transfer to disc. Inter's own processing facilities are also available for material of the higher visual quality than developers might other produce on their own desktop systems.

DVI technology now involves plug-in boards for the computer (PC or Macintosh), but should eventually be miniaturised to a single chip on the computer's motherboard. However, rapid developments in other areas mean that DVI technology is now only one of a number of options for computer users who want to incorporate still and moving video on the desktop.

Acorn Replay

Acorn Replay is an audio and video replay system implemented in software only. As with DVI technology, the audio-visual material may be created through conventional media, and then processed for storage on CD by authorised Compression Service Providers (CSPs). CSPs use Acorn's compression software with high-quality video editing equipment to transfer the video into Acorn Replay format. Once the material is returned to the developer, the Replay material can be integrated into various applications, and incorporated in learning material through the use of authoring systems.

The Replay material can be played back at 25 frames per second (fps) to support full-motion video within one-quarter of the screen on the Acorn Archimedes ARM3 powered computers (i.e. A540 and A5000). The ARM2 Acorn Archimedes machines (e.g. A440 and A3000) can play similar movies back at 12.5 fps. Acorn is using the mass storage of CD-ROM to store the compressed video and audio.

The use of Acorn Replay movies within authoring systems requires more memory. A11 A5000 with 2MB of RAM running in screen mode 15 can play packets created in Magpie, for instance, which contain moving images. However, to run in screen mode 28 and create packages requires a minimum of 4MB of RAM in the computer.

AppleQuickTime

QuickTime, launched in 1992, is now part of the system software of all new Apple computers – the compression software sits within the computer's operating system so that developers and users can employ moving pictures stored and processed through QuickTime without being aware of the program which supports this facility. Moving images sitting in Word or PageMaker files, for instance, need to refer to the QuickTime extension in the system folder, and a copy of the application with which the file was created, but end-users will not be aware of QuickTime as a specific element of the display.

QuickTime can be used on its own, or with third-party products: for instance, a Macintosh with a video spigot card (that displays digital video on the computer screen) in the computer and QuickTime in the system file, can capture images and store them on the hard disk. Programs such as Screen Play can be used to capture the video from tape, and many third party products to capture, process and display QuickTime video are now coming onto the market.

QuickTime, like Acorn Replay, is still restricted to a partial-screen display within a window, and speeds lower than full-motion at 25 fps are certainly faster and easily to process and display. Unlike Replay, QuickTime video can be created and processed entirely by the developer or even end-user.

Microsoft's Video for Windows

Video for Windows – originally called Audio/Video Interleave (AVI) – is a compression facility developed by Microsoft for the PC environment, which offers facilities similar to those in Replay and QuickTime.

Given the vast number of PCs in business, industry, homes and schools, this technology has the potential to set a *de facto* standard like that of the PC itself, simply by capturing this huge waiting market. Even fast and powerful PCs in the 486 range are now competing for a share of the home computer market and, with the recent 'price wars', PCs and their clones represent both a cost-effective option and the *de facto* industry standard. There is considerable anecdotal evidence from both schools and computer dealers and manufacturers that many institutions are buying PCs (or clones) for their attractive price, powerful features, wide range of complementary software programs and hardware options – and because the PC is the machine which students are most likely to encounter when they enter the workforce.

Conclusion

Thus, Video for Windows could prove an attractive option for colleges, which are already tied to PCs. However, as the discussion above suggests, other technologies are developing rapidly, and PC users now have a wide range of choice for products of all kinds. The future of all these standards and technologies is largely a watching breed, as some degree of market 'shakedown' is inevitable with so many new products competing for attention.

References

Catt M. & Hirst G. (1990) An intelligent CALL system for grammatical error diagnosis, *Computer Assisted Language Learning*, **3**, 3-26, Oxford UK: Intellect.

City & Guilds (1991) *Vocational Language Schemes (January) Record of Performance Book*, City and Guilds of London Institute, 76 Portland Place, London W1N 4AA.

Department of Employment (1990) *Educational Technology in Modern Languages*, A report prepared by University of East Anglia and the Bell Educational Trust.

Department of Employment (1992) *New Perspectives in Modern Language Learning*, A report prepared by University of East Anglia.

DES/WO/HMSO (1990a) *Modern Foreign Languages in the National Curriculum*, March.

DES/WO/HMSO (1990b) *Technology in the National Curriculum, March.*

Dulay, M. and Burt, H. (1977) Remarks on Creativity in Language Acquisition, in *Viewpoints on English as a Second Language*, M. Burt, H. Dulay, M. Finnochiaro (eds) Regent's, New York, p. 95-126.

Dulay, M. and Burt, H. (1978) Some Guidelines for the Assessment of Oral Language Proficiency and Dominance, *TESOL Quarterly* **12**(2), 177-192.

Embleton, D. & Hagen, S. (eds) (1992) *Languages in International Business. A Practical Guide*, London: Hodder & Stoughton, April.

Goddard, A. and Harding, J. (1991) Languages Resources Room, in *Languages for Life: Modern Technologies*, Gele, M. and Little, J. (eds), Norfolk Educational Press, Norfolk.

Goodison, T. (1990) Interactive Video in the Classroom, *Language Learning Journal*, (UK) September, 68-70.

Hagen, S. (ed) (1988) *Languages in British Business. An Analysis of Current Needs*, London: CILT & Newcastle: Unique Publishers, Northumbria University.

Higgins, J. (1988) *Language, Learners and Computers*, London: Longman.

Hill, B. (1991) *Making the Most of Satellites and Interactive Video*, London: CILT.

Kempen G. (1991) Second Language Acquisition as a Hybrid Learning Process, in *Educational Technology, Cognitive Modelling and Interactive Environments*, Bouwhuis, D. & Engel, F. (eds), Heidelberg: Springer Verlag.

Kornum, L. (1990) Interactive Video in Denmark, *Language Learning Journal*, (UK) March, 52-54.

Krashen, S. (1981) Effective Second Language Acquisition: Insights from Research, in *The Second Language Classroom: Directions for the 1980s,* Alatis, J., Altman, H., Alatis, M. (eds), NY: OUP.

Krashen, S. (1985) *Language Acquisition and Language Education,* London: Prentice Hall International.

Lelouch R. (1991) Using multiple knowledge bases to help teach some pragmatic aspect of French, *Computer Assisted Language Learning* 4(1), 29-40, Oxford UK: Intellect.

Little, D. (ed) (1989) *Self-access Systems for Language Learning*, CILT, London.

Manning, P. (1990) *Methodological Considerations in the Design of CALL Programs*, Open University CITE report No. 131.

Marullo, G. and Laurillard, D. (1990) *An adaptive tutoring system for second language learning,* Open University CITE report No. 130.

NALA (1989) *Equipping the Modern Languages Department for the 1990s,* the National Association of Language Advisers, 19 High Street, Eccleshall, Stafford.

NCC (1992) *Modern Foreign Languages: non-statutory guidance*, National Curriculum Council, York.

NCET Report (1991) *Language Training for Industry: The Role of Open Learning*, Coventry:The National Council for Educational Technology.

Pijls F., Daelemans W., & Kempen G. (1987) Artificial intelligence tools for grammar and spelling instruction, *Instructional Science*, **16**, 319-336, Dordrecht: Kluwer.

Stevick, E. (1976) Memory, Meaning and Method, Rowley, MA: Newbury House.

Swartz, M.J., Kostyla, S.J., Hanfling, S., & Holland, V.M. (1990) Preliminary assessment of a foreign language learning environment, *Computer Assisted Language Learning*, **1**, 51-64, Oxford UK: Intellect.

Training Agency Report (1990) *Educational Technology in Modern Language Learning. A Report for the Training Agency*, Moorfoot, Sheffield, UK, prepared by University of East Anglia.

Tumber, M. (1991) Developing Pupil Autonomy, *Language Learning Journal*, (UK) September, p. 24-26.

Twidale, M., Pengelly, M., Chanier, T., and Self, J. (1990) Experiments on knowledge acquisition for learner modelling, in *Proceedings of DELTA and Beyond Conference*, Den Haag: Holland.

Wenger, E. (1987) *Artificial Intelligence and Tutoring Systems*, Los Altos, Ca.: Morgan Kaufmann Publishers Inc.

Wright, L.M. (1992) Designing and constructing a voice card language laboratory, *Computer Assisted Language Learning*, 5(3), 159-164.